P9-CKD-597

critical essays in modern literature

critical essays in modern literature

james
agee

818.5
Ag32s

james agee

promise and fulfillment

by kenneth seib

111760

LIBRARY ST. MARY'S COLLEGE

WITHDRAWN

university of pittsburgh press

The discussion of *A Death in the Family* in Chapter IV appears
in somewhat different form as a STUDY*MASTER® Publication
by Kenneth Seib entitled *A Death in the Family: A Critical
Commentary.* Copyright 1965 American R.D.M. Corporation.
All rights to this section of the present book are reserved by
American R.D.M. Corporation.

*Grateful acknowledgement is made to the following for
permission to quote material which appears in this book:*

James Agee Trust, for quotations from "Six Days at Sea,"
in *Fortune,* September, 1937.

John Updike, for quotations from "No Use Talking." Copyright ©
1962 by John Updike in *Assorted Prose,* published by
Alfred A. Knopf, Inc., New York. "No Use Talking" originally
appeared in the August 13, 1962 issue of *The New Republic.*

George Braziller, Inc., for quotations from *The Letters of
James Agee to Father Flye,* by James Agee.

Life, for quotations from "A Cult Grew Around a Many–Sided
Writer," by Richard Oulahan.

Random House, Inc., for quotations from "Death of a Poet"
in *Against the American Grain,* by Dwight Macdonald.
Copyright © 1957 by Dwight Macdonald. "Death of a Poet"
was originally published in the November 16, 1957 issue
of *The New Yorker.*

Houghton Mifflin Company, for quotations from *Let Us
Now Praise Famous Men,* by James Agee and Walker Evans.
Copyright © 1960 by Walker Evans. Reprinted by permission
of the publisher, Houghton Mifflin Company.

Grosset & Dunlap, Inc., for quotations from *A Death in
the Family,* by James Agee. Copyright © 1958 James Agee
Trust. Permission granted by the publisher, Grosset & Dunlap
Inc. And for quotations from *Agee on Film: Reviews and
Comments,* Vols. I and II. Copyright © 1957 McDowell &
Obolensky. Permission granted by the publisher, Grosset
& Dunlap, Inc.

Library of Congress Catalog Card Number: 68-21634
Copyright © 1968, University of Pittsburgh Press
Manufactured in the United States of America

*To my mother, whose death
in my family taught me
more about living*

preface

James Agee died in 1955, a man, as Dwight Macdonald claimed, "spectacularly born in the wrong time and place." A writer of awesome versatility, Agee still seems spectacularly out of place, for he failed to supply critics with a neat little bundle of poems or novels that could be unraveled by modern critical expertise. He wrote too little and, at the same time, too much. His mind played freely over wide areas, and categories fail to enclose him. He was always a poet, but he wrote relatively little poetry. He had a natural bent for fiction, but he produced only one full-length novel. He was a sensitive critic, but he spent his energies flailing away at grade B movies. Consequently, and for lack of anything else to say about him, some commentators discard him in that vast graveyard of American authors whose promise was never fulfilled, and James Agee shares a common grave with such spectres as Harold Frederic, Thomas Wolfe, and Vachel Lindsay.

Like that of composer Gustav Mahler, however, Agee's time seems about to come. Published criticism about Agee consists at the moment of one book and several scattered articles. There is no major biography and no *explication du text* of such complex works as *Let Us Now Praise Famous Men* or *A Death in the Family*. What is needed, therefore, is a guide to all of Agee's published writings, an introduction to the works which now comprise his canon. This book is meant to be that introduction, and I hope that the reader will consider it in this light. Since Agee is still largely unknown to the general reading public, I thought an opening biographical chapter necessary. It by no means pretends to be an exhaustive account of Agee's life; it is intended merely to give the reader some biographical details to go on. In chapter two, I have quoted rather heavily, for it is unlikely that most readers are familiar with Agee's poetry. Finally, chapter five is a general outline of Agee's thinking about the cinema; little more could be done, in the allotted space, with the rich but unwieldy body of his film criticism. I hope to see, in the future, an entire book devoted to Agee's film work. It is possible, the reader should be aware, that all of the Agee canon is not yet in, for there are rumors of other manuscripts yet unpublished. Any final evaluation of Agee's total body of writings, therefore, is subject to change.

I am heavily indebted to many people for their assistance in preparing this book. My special thanks, however, must go to Dr. Robert Gale of the University of Pittsburgh who guided, red-penciled, and prodded my ideas into existence. But I absolve Dr. Gale of all guilt, for the ideas and their expression are solely my own responsibility. I would also like to thank Study*Master Publications for allowing me to use material that I had originally published for them. Finally, I am deeply grateful to my wife Jane for, among other things, proofreading, criticism, and unflagging confidence.

Harrogate, England   K. S.
April, 1968

contents

james
agee

promise

*The roots are emotion and
intuitiveness; the chief necessity
is discipline.*
—*Agee,* Letters to Father Flye

i

Some critics claim that James Agee
just missed greatness. Had he not wasted his genius in
Hollywood and on commercial magazines, they say, he
might have become the greatest novelist or poet of
his generation. But such criticism misses the point. Randall
Jarrell said that a "good poet is someone who manages,
in a lifetime of standing out in thunderstorms, to be
struck by lightning five or six times; a dozen or two dozen
times and he is great."[1] Agee, standing in thunderstorms,
was struck by lightning five or six times, but each time
by a bolt from a different Muse—a fact which confuses
all definitions of "good" and "great" and points out
Agee's uniqueness. In his short lifetime he produced a
volume of poetry, a novel, a book on southern tenant
farming, countless film reviews, several film scripts and
short works of fiction, and numerous letters. Agee's
greatness, therefore, is not conventional, for the quality of
his work is spread throughout half a dozen different
genres. A great writer, James Agee confounds our
traditional notions of greatness.

Agee, by temperament, was an eighteenth-century man of letters. His was one of those minds that could change directions smoothly and quickly from the marketplace to the ivory tower without a loss of momentum or power. He threw his talents into popular media and serious art, and was equally accomplished in both, refusing to dash off uninspired performances with his left hand. Agee was, as Alfred Kazin has claimed, "a writer who gave all of himself, and often it was himself literally that he gave, to every medium that he worked in—poetry, fiction, reportage, criticism, movies, television. He was not only one of the most gifted writers in the United States, but such a natural as a writer that he found a creative opportunity in every place where drearier people pitied themselves for potboiling."[2] As Robert Phelps has said, Agee was "a born, sovereign prince of the English language."[3]

James Rufus Agee was born in Knoxville, Tennessee, on November 27, 1909. His last name, puzzling to many readers, is pronounced, Father Flye tells us, by saying quickly the letters A-G and putting a strong accent on the A.[4] Aware of this problem in pronunciation, Agee mentions it in one of his frequent writings about himself, a humorous autobiography written in the third person: "He does not like to be called Aggie, Uh*gee,* Egg-*gee,* Ag-*yow,* or Rufus. 'Don't call me that.' he says."[5] It is evident from his letters to Father Flye that he was known to at least some of his friends as Rufus. As late as 1948 he was signing his name both "Jim" and "Rufus." If we consider the portrait of Rufus Follet in *A Death in the Family* to be a partial portrait of the artist himself—and it is impossible not to—we get a vivid picture of the humiliation felt by young Rufus because of his name. Tricked into revealing his name to the older boys on the block, Rufus "had come almost to feel that

the name itself was being physically hurt, and he did
not want it to be hurt again. . . ."

And the instant it was out of his mouth he knew that
he had been mistaken once again, that not a single soul
of them had meant one thing that he had said, for with that
instant every one of them screamed as loudly as he could
with a ferocious kind of joy, and it was as if the whole
knot exploded and sent its fragments tearing all over
the neighborhood, screaming his name with amusement
and apparently with some kind of contempt; and many
of them screamed, as well, a verse which they seemed to
think very funny, though Rufus could not understand
why.

 Uh-Rufus, Uh-Rastus, Uh-Johnson, Uh-Brown,

 uh-What ya gonna do when the rent comes roun?
and others yelled, "Nigger's name, nigger's name," and
chanted a verse that he had often heard them yell after
the backs of colored children and even grown-up colored
people,

> Nigger, nigger, black as tar,
> Tried to ride a lectric car,
> Car broke down an broke his back
> Poor nigger wanted his nickel back.

Three or four, instead of running, stood screaming his
name and those verses at him, and the word, "nigger,"
jumping up and down and shoving their fingers at his
chest and stomach and face while he stood in abashment,
and followed by these, he would walk unhappily home.[6]

The most important event of Agee's childhood occurred
when he was six years old: his father, Hugh James Agee,
died. For the remainder of his life, there was something
of Telemachus in James Agee—as there is, perhaps,
in all men. But any attempt at psychological analysis

LIBRARY ST. MARY'S COLLEGE

proves futile, for it took Agee thirty years to discover his complex reactions to his father's death. Our major concern should be that his discoveries resulted in *A Death in the Family*.

After the death of his father, Agee spent his remaining childhood visiting relatives and pursuing an education. It was during one of his early wanderings that Agee met Father James Harold Flye, an Episcopalian priest, who became not only a close friend but a spiritual adviser as well. In 1919 Agee's mother took a summer cottage near St. Andrew's, a school for boys about two miles from Sewanee, Tennessee. She decided to stay for the following winter, and she enrolled her two children, James and Emma, in local schools. James—or Rufus, as he was then called—went to St. Andrew's and stayed for several years, making intermittent visits during summers and on holidays to the home of his mother's parents in Knoxville. According to Father Flye, a teacher at St. Andrew's during Agee's stay, the school "was then, as it is now, under the direction of a monastic order in the Episcopal Church, the Order of the Holy Cross: a little school community in the country, on the Cumberland Plateau, having at that time some ninety pupils from the primary grades up through high school. Visitors and people from the neighborhood often came to Sunday services in the chapel; the religious tone was strong and pervasive, but of a friendly, natural and unaffected quality, far removed from anything of piousness or stuffiness."[7]

The friendship between Father Flye and Agee, begun at St. Andrew's in 1919, lasted until 1955, the year of Agee's death. In Father and Mrs. Flye, Agee found the familial love he had lost through the death of his father. He began to study French outside school with Father Flye, and at the age of sixteen he made with Father Flye his only trip to Europe. There, as he wrote later, he "explored the 'slums,' watched out for American moving pictures, and climbed the cathedrals."[8]

In the fall of 1925 Agee entered Phillips Exeter Academy in New Hampshire, where his literary ambitions, perhaps inspired by Father Flye, began to take form. "I have written stuff for the *Monthly* [Phillips Exeter's literary publication]," he wrote to Father Flye in 1925, "and I am to get a story and 2 or 3 poems in this month."[9] These early endeavors, however, may have been more for social than for literary conquests, for he adds that such publication will get him into the Lantern Club, a campus literary organization, "one of the big things to be in here."[10] "I'm sending a copy of the *Monthly* down," he wrote to Father Flye the following year. "I have a play in, which is more or less the result of St. Andrew's."[11] In subsequent letters, Agee mentions a a play called *Catched,* a "mountaineer play," and another called *Menalcas* ("my Greek play"), which was read and praised by Robert Frost.[12] He discloses, too, that he had written, at the age of eighteen, a 500-line poem "about a lady named Ann Garner."[13] The Ann Garner poem appeared later, in more polished form, in *Permit Me Voyage.*

One finds, also, in these youthful letters, Agee's increasing awareness of himself as a human being and an artist. "You know, since last winter or so," he wrote in 1927, "I've been feeling something—a sort of universal —oh, I don't know, feeling the beauty of everything, not excluding slop-jars and foetuses—and a feeling of love for everything—and now I've run into Walt Whitman— and it seems as if I'd dived into a sort of infinitude of beautiful stuff—all the better (for me) because it was just what has been knocking at me unawares."[14] It is precisely this love of everything, "not excluding slop-jars and foetuses," that marks Agee's mature work and sets him apart from most of his generation of writers.

In the autumn of 1928 Agee entered Harvard for what he considered "the four happiest years of his life."[15] His Harvard years were not particularly distinguished, and he entered his senior year with the vague feeling that he wanted to write, "probably poetry in the main."[16] Two other chief interests, music and motion picture directing, had "slowly been killed off, partly by brute and voluntary force," but mainly by his desire to write.[17] With customary undergraduate caution, however, he aspired at this point to become no more than a very minor writer. "My intellectual pelvic girdle," he wrote to Father Flye, "simply is not Miltonically wide."[18]

During his final year at Harvard in 1932, Agee wrote a parody of *Time* magazine, which, along with a recommendation from Dwight Macdonald, resulted in a job offer as a cub reporter for *Fortune*. He accepted the position and worked for *Fortune* until 1939. For a young man with poetic ambitions, an excursion into the world of commercial journalism must have seemed like a destructive compromise. He admitted to friends that he was working "in a whorehouse."[19] On the other hand, "there was also no doubt," W. M. Frohock points out, "that he took great satisfaction in concocting, out of the most recalcitrant technical materials, what have to be called masterpieces of that kind of journalism."[20] There is, at any rate, a noticeable change of tone between his Harvard letters and his later correspondence with Father Flye. His university work, he wrote in December, 1931, had been "going *continuously* at top speed—mind, body, and nerves . . . with powers, pain, and joy all humming at once; with everything at once terrifically actual, yet abstracted and clear as glass: even dull and microscopic things seemed magnificently alive and exciting: and very little was dull and microscopic."[21] The following letter, dated eight months later, shortly after Agee had started working for *Fortune*, is a painful contrast: "If I am, as I seem to be, dying on my feet mentally and spiritually, and can do nothing about it, I'd prefer not to know I was dying . . . I've felt like suicide for weeks now—and not just fooling with the idea, but feeling seriously on the edge of it."[22] "I simply am not capable," he concluded, "of being the kind of person, doing the kind of things, which I want to be."[23]

Although obviously unhappy when writing what he termed "Pay Dirt," Agee hurled himself with uncommon zeal into his *Fortune* assignments. "I've been extremely busy on an article on machine-made rugs," he revealed to Father Flye in 1932.[24] In following years he wrote an article on the Tennessee Valley Authority, another about interior decorating, and a piece on orchids.[25] Concerned with mundane matters, he found little time for more literary efforts. Only one lucid article that he wrote for *Fortune* approaches literary stature, an unsigned story titled "Six Days at Sea," which Richard Oulahan describes as "an acid scrutiny of the passengers aboard a cruise ship bound for Havana."[26]

In 1934 Agee's only volume of poetry, *Permit Me Voyage,* appeared in print with a laudatory foreword by Archibald MacLeish. Two years later, in the summer of 1936, Agee and photographer Walker Evans spent eight weeks in Alabama, assigned by *Fortune* to do a series of articles on tenant families and rural economics in the South. From this experience Agee later wrote *Let Us Now Praise Famous Men,* a torrent of intensely moving poetic prose. The book, eventually published in 1941, was a commercial failure but a critical success. This was essentially all the writing of quality that Agee produced between 1932 and 1939. By the end of this period he felt that he had "missed irretrievably all the trains [he] should have caught."[27]

How seriously did Agee's commercial writing damage his artistic ability? The question is basic to any serious study of his life and works, and many critics have already reached a largely erroneous judgment. All of Agee's writings, W. M. Frohock concludes, "bring home to the reader a realization of what this man could have left behind if his great gift had not been channeled off in other directions. If he had 'kept his promise' by writing what was expected of him instead of what he most wanted to write, he would have had his paragraph in the histories of fiction."[28] This essentially unclear and illogical statement will be discussed in the final chapter. The problem, briefly, involves more than "unkept promise" or mere prostitution to a bourgeois commercialism. Agee was his own worst enemy, hell-bent on self-destruction and shamefully irresponsible about his own talent. Added to this was what he admittedly called "a dirty and unconquerable vein of melancholia in me."[29] It was a melancholy composed of an awareness of his own extravagance, a hill-country *Weltschmerz* stemming from his Tennessee background and religious upbringing, and, at times, a conscious Byronic posturing. The problem is further complicated by the fact that Agee was laboring in a mass culture media which the professional literary establishment had taught its public to scorn.

Even if Agee had slipped the confines of the Luce syndicate, it is debatable whether he would have produced a larger body of great literature. His chief need, as he realized, was not greater freedom, but further discipline:

Without guidance, balance, coordination, my ideas and impressions and desires, which are much larger than I can

begin to get to paper, are loose in my brains like wild
beasts of assorted sizes and ferocities, not devouring each
other but in the process of tearing the zoo to parts. Or
more accurately like the feeling they are loose wires highly
charged which cross and short-circuit and send burning
spasms all through me, with nothing connecting long
enough to hold, and give power or light. The wise answer
of course would be that there is only one coordinator
and guide, and that he is come at through self-negation.
But: that can mean nothing to me until or unless I learn
it for myself. Without scrupulousness I am damned
forever, and my base, if I ever find it, must be of my
own finding and understanding or it is no sort of base at
all. Well, it cannot be solved.[30]

That he did solve it was Agee's triumph as a writer. Other
writers, searching for mythologies, tradition, and individual
talent, failed to achieve the synthesis of compassion,
artistry, and control that Agee attained through hard work
and integrity. Eschewing escapism and expatriation,
Agee eventually found the discipline that equally talented
artists—Thomas Wolfe, for example—lacked.

In the 1940's Agee wrote copy for *Time* magazine,
including feature articles on the death of President
Roosevelt and the bombing of Hiroshima; he also wrote
motion picture reviews for the *Nation*. The latter job
stimulated his imagination, for he always had more than
the average American's love for motion pictures. Soon
Agee's film reviews gained for their writer a minor,
yet national, reputation: they were clear, balanced,
entertaining, well-written. Moreover, he was attempting
to formulate a critical method for judging the cinema as
an art form.

Agee in 1942 was living modestly in what he described
as "a little 'flat' in Cornelia Street, in the Italian, not the

Anglo-Bohemian, quarter of 'The Village.' "[31] Dwight
Macdonald remembers him during this time as an
"extraordinary self-destructive" man who "was always
ready to sit up all night with anyone who happened to be
around, or to go out at midnight looking for someone:
talking passionately, brilliantly, but too much, drinking
too much, smoking too much, reading aloud too much,
making love too much, and in general cultivating the
worst set of work habits in Greenwich Village."[32] Other
friends recall him as a sort of combination Abraham
Lincoln and Li'l Abner, a man whose deepest nature was
grounded in melancholy and whose physical appearance
contained a rude, gentle, and endearing hill-country
simplicity. According to Walker Evans:

> He didn't look much like a poet, an intellectual, an
> artist, or a Christian, each of which he was. Nor was
> there outward sign of his paralyzing, self-lacerating
> anger. His voice was pronouncedly quiet and lowpitched,
> though not of "cultivated" tone. It gave the impression
> of diffidence, but never of weakness. His accent was
> more or less unplaceable and it was somewhat variable.
> For instance, in Alabama it veered towards
> country-southern, and I may say he got away with
> this to the farm families and to himself.
> His clothes were deliberately cheap, not only
> because he was poor but because he wanted to be
> able to forget them. He would work a suit into fitting
> him perfectly by the simple method of not taking it
> off much. In due time the cloth would mold itself to
> his frame. Cleaning and pressing would have undone
> this beautiful process. I exaggerate, but it did seem
> sometimes that wind, rain, work, and mockery were his
> tailors. On another score, he felt that wearing good,
> expensive clothes involved him in some sort of claim to

superiority of the social kind. Here he occasionally
confused his purpose, and fell over into a knowingly
comical inverted dandyism. He got more delight out of
factory-seconds sneakers and a sleazy cap than a
straight dandy does from waxed calf Peal shoes and a
brushed Lock & Co. bowler.[33]

All who attempt to describe the man claim that words
fail to depict Agee. There was something mythical in
his personality that eluded analysis.

The outbreak of World War II further complicated
Agee's view of the world and of himself. Classified 4-F
in the draft, he saw himself as an "armchair anarchist."[34]
His liberal leanings were clearly Socialist rather than
Communist, and they stemmed from a wish for world
brotherhood rather than from a desire for violent
overthrow of existing government. He loved democracy
rationally and open-mindedly, refusing to be caught up
in thoughtless patriotic fervor. The concept of war itself,
and the killing and destruction that go along with it,
was abhorrent to him. "The only positive feeling I have
for being in [the war]," he said, "is really a negative
one—that in one single respect it is not happy to be out
of a thing in which so many are suffering. But that is
as much as I can conceivably feel in its favor."[35] Agee
spent the war years writing short-lived articles for the
Luce organization.

When the war ended, Agee seemed to gain new vitality.
"I've started a short novel about adolescence in the
1920's," he wrote to Father Flye in 1945.[36] This short
novel, published six years later, was *The Morning Watch*.
In 1946 he wrote a long verse letter to Father Flye.
In 1948 he started another novel, "about my first 6 years,
ending the day of my father's burial," which ultimately
became *A Death in the Family*.[37]

During this period, also, Agee's private life became less chaotic than usual. In 1946 he married Mia Fritsch, after previous unsuccessful marriages to Olivia Saunders and Alma Mailman, and lived happily with her until his death. He already had a son named Joel by his second wife, and Mia gave him two more children, Julia Teresa and John Alexander.

By the late forties Agee was working in a new medium —motion pictures. In 1948 he wrote the commentary for Helen Levitt's poignant film *The Quiet One,* a documentary about a young Negro's attempt to adjust to a hostile world. Later in that same year he wrote two film scripts based on Stephen Crane short stories, "The Blue Hotel" and "The Bride Comes to Yellow Sky." In 1950 he worked with John Huston, who became a close friend, on the script of C. S. Forester's *The African Queen.* Two years later he was commissioned by the Ford Foundation to write a television script on the life of Lincoln. This successful and highly praised program was further distinguished in that Agee himself played one of the prominent roles. In 1954 he wrote the screenplay for *The Night of the Hunter,* a high-quality horror film, and worked on the script of *Noa Noa,* a film (never produced) that was to be based on the South Sea diary of Paul Gauguin.

During the period 1945–1955 Agee worked tirelessly. His creative powers were at their peak, his works were getting published, and either through circumstance or through sheer hard work, his misgivings and melancholia had given way and cleared his mind of past obstacles. He wanted to do everything at once: novels, film scripts, poetry, short stories. He often went without sleep (he suffered, too, from insomnia), bolstering himself with alcohol in order to accomplish his writing projects. Despite his seemingly inexhaustible energy, his body finally broke

down in 1951. Three successive attacks of pain in his
chest, teeth, and forearms which disabled him in January
were diagnosed as a coronary thrombosis. He was ordered
to spend a month in the hospital. In November he had
another attack and again was hospitalized. Other attacks
followed. "I've been finding more and more constant
awareness of death, and the shortness of time, and of time
wasted," he wrote in 1954.[38] But he refused to take care
of himself, and he threw himself again into a variety
of projects. "I'm working this week," he wrote to Father
Flye in 1954, "developing an outline of a story for a
movie about musicians in Tanglewood, Mass. It could, I
think, be good, and it will, I think, be made. Many other
jobs, embryonic, or hanging fire: my own story, here:
The Naked and the Dead; a movie about Heine; a
television series about crime to be made in Hollywood—
but, as always, things take forever to crystallize, and
one can count for nothing."[39] During this period he was
also working on his Gauguin screenplay and on *A Death
in the Family*. Richard Oulahan describes these last few
years:

If he had taken care of himself, Agee might have lived
for 15 or 20 years more. In his brief years, he pushed
himself inhumanly. He suffered from insomnia, and filled
in the morning watches with drinking and conversation.
Movie director John Huston, an early Agee admirer and
collaborator, recalls that he "was one of those fellows
who never said no to anyone." When Huston and Agee
were working on the script of *The African Queen*
in California, Huston suggested a strenuous health
routine, with violent exercise, a minimum of drinking
and lots of sun, during the days. Agee agreed to the
daytime regimen, but spent his nights drinking and
turning out hundreds of pages of script in his tiny

handwriting. The strain brought on a serious heart attack. When Huston was permitted to visit him in the hospital, Agee immediately asked for a cigaret. Huston had to refuse, and tried to explain that Agee had had a narrow escape and would have to change his way of life drastically. Jim reflected for a moment, then replied, "Well, I wouldn't want to change my way of life." Many months later, in New York, the two men met again. "Jim was living just as he always had," Huston says. "I knew then that it was just a question of time." If Agee had obeyed the doctor's orders, he might have prolonged his life. He might have gone on like Maurice Utrillo, begrudgingly bringing forth sterile new works of art, but his heart would not have been in it, and Agee was above all else a writer with heart.[40]

On May 11, 1955, Agee wrote to Father Flye: "I feel, in general, as if I were dying: a terrible slowing-down, in all ways, above all else in relation to work."[41] Five days later, while riding in a New York taxi, Agee died of a heart attack.

James Agee's finest work, *A Death in the Family,* which was published shortly after his death, won a Pulitzer Prize. In 1961 it became a successful Broadway play, adapted by Tad Mosel, called *All The Way Home.* In 1963 it was made into a motion picture, with the screenplay written by Philip Reisman, Jr. In 1962 a collection of Agee's letters appeared, and there is a possibility of more work to be published. According to Richard Oulahan, "McDowell [Agee's publisher] discovered two unpublished chapters of *A Death in the Family* stuffed into an old copy of *Time.* They will be printed eventually. Robert Fitzgerald, an associate of Agee's on *Time,* is editing a new edition of his poetry, including a dozen unpublished portions of *Let Us Now*

Praise Famous Men. McDowell is working on a biography, and gathering another selection of the Agee letters. And perhaps, in the untidy trunks and desk drawers Agee left, there might be another *Death in the Family*."[42] Dwight Macdonald can recall "grocery cartons full of manuscripts [Agee] had put aside."[43]

The epitome of the artist struggling in a commercial society, Agee has attracted a number of followers. Much like devotees of the late movie actor James Dean, Agee's admirers are too often attracted to the myth and are oblivious to the artist's merits and failures. The Agee cult has arisen, according to Dwight Macdonald, "partly because of the power of his writing and his lack of recognition—everyone likes to think he is on to a good thing the general public has not caught up with—but mainly it is felt that Agee's life and personality, like Dean's, were at once a symbolic expression of our time and a tragic protest against it. It is felt that not their weakness but their vitality betrayed them. In their maimed careers and their wasteful deaths, the writer and the actor appeal to a resentment that intellectuals and teen-agers alike feel about life in America, so smoothly prosperous, so deeply frustrating."[44]

Whether Agee was "betrayed" is debatable. Like so many writers before him, he died while his artistic powers were near or at their peak, and it is tempting to claim that in some subtle way Agee was another American Adam betrayed by a serpentine and "smoothly prosperous" society. To see James Agee merely as a writer of "unkept promise," as a creative artist lured to destruction, like the Lady of Shalott, by commercial tinsel and glitter, is to belittle his distinguished achievements. Rather than a victim of society, Agee was a product of his society. In an age that was evolving new media of expression such as television and elevating others such as reportage and motion pictures to unprecedented levels of national importance, Agee was truly an avant-garde artist. He viewed the motion picture, for example, with a scholar's seriousness before it was fashionable to do so, and he wrote experimental drama for television in the days when literate tv drama was still a possibility. He wrote a book which was, and still is, an unclassifiable oddity, and he brought the poetic potentiality of English prose to a level unsurpassed by any of his contemporaries. In an age of specialization and fragmentation, James Agee was a total writer, a professional who earned his living solely by his pen. In short, Agee fulfilled his promise, but in his own way, after a long search and after abandoning many modes of expression, and he fulfilled it in a manner peculiar to an American writer of the post-thirties. That he was denied the final accolade of his time is merely further indication that James Agee, like all great writers, was both of his time and ahead of it.

the failure
of form

*Make the eyes of our hearts, and
the voice of our hearts in speech,
honest and lovely within the fences
of our nature, and a little clear.*
—*Agee,* Permit Me Voyage

James Agee began to write poetry at
Phillips Exeter Academy, and despite the publication of
only one volume of verse and a few short poems, he
continued to write poetry all of his life. He was a natural
poet: all of his writings reveal an instinct for exact
words, striking images, detailed observations, and
rhythmical lines. His poetry is intensely lyrical, and at its
core is a vein of melancholy and a universal concern with
the mutability of love, human relationships, and existence.
In addition, it is a specifically American poetry;
although no Frost or Sandburg, Agee harbored an
almost mystical love for America's history, tradition, and
people. Why his poetry has made little impression upon
the poetry-reading public, therefore, is at first slightly
puzzling. Early reviewers of *Permit Me Voyage*
bestowed either mild encouragement or meaningless
platitudes, while later critics lamented Agee's wasted
poetic talent. All fail to consider his actual achievement.

Agee's poetry, strangely conservative in style, blatantly
romantic in subject matter, and peculiarly religious in
tone, often seems a prelude to something that never came.

The fusion of fresh idiom and complex meaning that
Agee so earnestly pursued generally fails to come through
in his poetry; the powerful surge of great verse, sweeping
beyond the barriers of mere technique, is too seldom
evident in *Permit Me Voyage*. As Archibald MacLeish
points out in the foreword, the book is the work "of a
young poet laboring at an art rather than the book of a
young poet laboring a distinction."[1]

"Words cannot embody; they can only describe," Agee
wrote in *Let Us Now Praise Famous Men:*

> But a certain kind of artist, whom we will distinguish from
> others as a poet rather than a prose writer, despises
> this fact about words of his medium, and continually
> brings words as near as he can to an illusion of embodiment
> In doing so he accepts a falsehood but makes, of a sort
> in any case, better art. It seems very possibly true that
> art's superiority over science and over all other forms of
> human activity, and its inferiority to them, reside in the
> identical fact that art accepts the most dangerous and
> impossible of bargains and makes the best of it, becoming,
> as a result, both nearer the truth and farther from it than
> those things which, like science and scientific art, merely
> describe, and those things which, like human beings and
> their creations and the entire state of nature, merely
> are, the truth.[2]

The reason Agee's poetry fails to satisfy completely i
found in the preceding passage. His artistic aim, like that
of the Realist school, was to approximate the "truth"
of physical experience. A work of art is not a
reconstruction of experience or a remembrance of things
past. A work of art *is* the experience, or, as Agee says,
it is "an illusion of embodiment." The poet, both adoring
and abhorring words and their limitations, goes beyond
the truth of science, which is solely descriptive and

analytical, and beyond the truth of things, which merely exist in and for themselves. The poet, in a rage for order, creates a world, and at the same time allows "truth" to radiate from that world. The poet's world both *is* and *means;* words should both embody *and* describe.

Another reason for dissatisfaction with Agee's poetry is that he chose to work almost slavishly within the limits of form, meter, and rhyme. Agee required the discipline of form to restrain his natural verbosity. But his poetry, as a result, is, as Dwight Macdonald states, "rather conventional and romantic."[3] *Permit Me Voyage* might have been more successful if Agee had been more daring. Such a statement, however, assumes that Agee would have been greater if he had not been who he was. It was simply not his way to throw discipline to the winds. Such freedom, he knew, would have been totally disastrous to an artist whose greatest problem was lack of discipline.

Nonetheless, Agee's poetry is a solid achievement, the work of a writer who has a genuine feeling for the sound and shape of words. His best poems are lyrical, intense, and kinetic, perfect examples of what Ezra Pound called "language charged with meaning to the utmost degree."[4] Two of the best examples of Agee's intense and energetic poetry, "Sunday: Outskirts of Knoxville, Tenn." and "Rapid Transit," did not appear in *Permit Me Voyage.* They came out in 1937, the Knoxville poem in *New Masses,* and "Rapid Transit," along with a poem entitled "Sun Our Father," in *Forum.* Both deserve close examination:

Rapid Transit

Squealing under city stone
    The millions on the millions run
Every one a life alone
    Every one a soul undone.

> There all the poisons of the heart
>   Branch and abound like whirling brooks
> And there through every useless art
>   Like spoiled meats on a butcher's hooks
>
> Pour forth upon their frightful kind
>   The faces of each ruined child:
> The wrecked demeanors of the mind
>   That now is tamed and once was wild.[5]

Although more didactic, "Rapid Transit" brings to mind
Pound's "In a Station of the Metro," as well as Hart
Crane's "Proem: To Brooklyn Bridge," in which
"bedlamites" scuttle from subways. The most precise and
startling image in Agee's poem is that of the faces of
the ruined city dwellers hanging like "spoiled meats on a
butcher's hooks," an image containing both accurate
description and moral condemnation of subway passengers.
More than an imagist poem, however, "Rapid Transit"
is colored by Agee's special vision, his hill-country dislike
of urban frenzy and his lifelong concern with the worth of
the individual.

Elizabeth Drew found "Sunday: Outskirts of Knoxville,
Tenn." a "masterly integration of sound and image
pattern woven and interwoven with the fabric of the verse"
and saw fit to give it a lengthy explication in *Directions
in Modern Poetry*.[6] The poem remains one of the best
introductions to Agee's evocative verse:

> *Sunday: Outskirts of Knoxville, Tenn.*
>
> There, in the earliest and chary spring, the
>   dogwood flowers.
>
> Unharnessed in the friendly sunday air
> By the red brambles, on the river bluffs,
> Clerks and their choices pair.

Thrive by, not near, masked all away by shrub
   and juniper,
The ford v eight, racing the chevrolet.

They can not trouble her:

Her breasts, helped open from the afforded lace,
Lie like a peaceful lake;
And on his mouth she breaks her gentleness:

Oh, wave them awake!

They are not of the birds. Such innocence
Brings us to break us only.
Theirs are not happy words.
We that are human cannot hope.
Our tenderest joys oblige us most.
No chain so cuts the bone; and sweetest silk
   most shrewdly strangles.

How this must end, that now please love were
   ended,
In kitchens, bedfights, silences, women's pages,
Sickness of heart before goldlettered doors,
Stale flesh, hard collars, agony in antiseptic
   corridors.
Spankings, remonstrances, fishing trips, orange
   juice,
Policies, incapacities, a chevrolet,
Scorn of their children, kind contempt exchanged,
Recalls, tears, second honeymoons, pity,
Shouted corrections of missed syllables,
Hot water bags, gallstones, falls down stairs,
Oldfashioned christmases, suspicions of theft,
Arrangements with morticians taken care of by
   sons in law,
Small rooms beneath the gables of brick bungalow,
The tumbler smashed, the glance between daughter
   and husband,

The empty body in the lonely bed
And, in the empty concrete porch, blown ash
Grandchildren wandering the betraying sun

Now, on the winsome crumbling shelves of the
    horror
God show, God blind these children![7]

Although it may seem verbose, "Sunday: Outskirts of
Knoxville, Tenn." is artistically deceptive. Like a
pointillist painting, it contains details that all lend meaning
to the total structure, while the words and sounds are
skillfully bound together. "There," "air," "pair," "near,"
"juniper," and "her" are interwoven into the first few
lines, and work on something other than a conscious level.
In the same way, "lace," "lake," "breaks," and "awake"
create a pattern of sound that one might easily miss.
As in most good poetry, the artistry lies hidden, giving one
the first impression that the poet is technically careless
and almost willfully naïve.

The poem breaks into two sections: the first ten lines,
which are descriptive of "chary spring," Sunday pleasures,
and pairing clerks and their choices; and the remaining
lines, which remind us of all the mortal frailties that
flesh is heir to. The dividing line is "Oh, wave them
awake!" The tension in the poem between daydreaming
ideals and waking reality is beautifully evoked by selected
experiences from an average lifetime: lovers' "bedfights,"
the agony of childbirth "in antiseptic corridors,"
"second honeymoons," the miseries of old age, and
finally the "empty body in the lonely bed." As the poet
ambiguously suggests, such horror would not happen if
God revealed to these innocents what is yet to come,
but in order for life to continue, He blinds them to the
ultimate outcome. The "shelves of horror" crumble either
way, Agee reminds us: "We that are human cannot hope."

This poem, as Elizabeth Drew states, "is a superlative example of the effectiveness of pattern. . . . Throughout, we are kept constantly aware of the two visions which compose the poem. The idyllic vision persists within the shadow of the realistic vision until the closing prayer brackets both. This dual vision is not sustained by means of direct reference but always by means of suggestion within the visual or sound pattern—a method which recalls Mallarmé's acknowledged aim, 'to evoke an object in deliberate shadow without ever actually mentioning it, by allusive words, never by direct words.' "[8]

Yet it is the Elizabethans, not the French symbolists, who first come to mind when one reads Agee's poetry. The lyric impulse, the grave and melodious phrase, and the metaphysical conceit pervade *Permit Me Voyage*. Agee even titles his poems with an Elizabethan simplicity: "Lyrics," "Epithalamium," and "Sonnets." One early poem, "The Passionate Poet to His Love," is a conscious imitation of Christopher Marlowe's "The Passionate Shepherd to His Love," while another, "Vertigral," has an alliterative obscurity reminiscent of late metaphysical verse. Finally, like that of the Elizabethans, the structure of Agee's poetry is often argumentative and the tone is frequently paradoxical. Yoking passion and intellect, Agee's verse seems closer to the Elizabethans than does that of other modern poets whose metaphysical borrowings have gained considerable commentary.

In addition, Hart Crane and Walt Whitman are the two most important and obvious American influences on Agee's verse. Agee borrowed much from Crane, including the title *Permit Me Voyage* from Crane's "Voyages III." A vivid clustering of image associations, syntactical complexity, and the persistent theme of the ecstasy and omnipotence of love, dominant qualities in Crane's work, dominate Agee's poetry. Like Crane and Whitman,

Agee was at odds with his society and believed that "science and scientific-quasi-ethical thought has brought something almost like destruction into love."[9] Again like Crane and Whitman, Agee had a penchant for detailed cataloging (see, for example, the "Dedication" to *Permit Me Voyage* or almost any page of *Let Us Now Praise Famous Men*), and he used a cumbersome rhetoric which, at its best, could achieve great intensity and energy. Finally, Agee had that same mystical affinity with the American soil that one finds in *Leaves of Grass* and *The Bridge*. "On the whole," critic Peter Ohlin summarizes, "it can be said that Agee's poetry, especially in *Permit Me Voyage,* exists in a field between two poles: one of them is the example of the sixteenth- and seventeenth-century Elizabethans, Donne, Shakespeare, and others; the other is provided by such American poets as Whitman and Hart Crane."[10]

Although it is difficult to detect any clear structural pattern to *Permit Me Voyage,* the opening poems, concerned with mutability and earthly frustrations, and the final devotional poems provide a clue. One can see the pattern of a spiritual quest for meaning in a world of fleeting values. The poems, in both tone and subject matter, move from earthly despair to spiritual acceptance. To insist on the presence of such structure, however, may be making too much of too little. It is more likely that the poems, broken up as they are into distinctive groups, stand separately.

"Lyrics" and "Dedication"

The opening poems of *Permit Me Voyage* are entitled merely "Lyrics," suggesting that they have a singing quality and are words set to imaginary music. Always meaningful in Agee's life, music proves influential in his verse. Like

Hart Crane in poems such as "Recitative," "Moment Fugue," and "Old Song," Agee envisioned much of his poetry in musical terms. It is noteworthy, too, that the first ten poems of this volume precede the dedication. Not out of place at all, they form a kind of overture, an introduction of major themes, to the remainder of the work. We find here the mutability of human life, deceit of lovers, frustrated ideals, and the glory of the creation— some of the themes that Agee returns to in later poems. *Permit Me Voyage,* in short, seems unified musically as well as substantively.

The opening poem is typical of Agee's lyrics:

> Child, should any pleasant boy
> Find you lovely, many could,
> Wind not up between your joy
> The sly delays of maidenhood;
> Spread all your beauty in his sight
> And do him kindness every way,
> Since soon, too soon, the wolfer night
> Climbs in between, and ends fair play.[11]

Writing to his coy mistress, the poet achieves a paradoxical tone. By advising this "child" (it is also possible that this child is indeed a child, making the tone instructive rather than seductive) to spread her beauty for some "pleasant boy," the poet reveals his own desire for the lady. Beneath this hymn to death and the maiden, there lurks the mild hope that the cruel fair's "sly delays of maidenhood" will be unwound for him. The last two lines, a skillful combination of the sensual and the ominous, is seventeenth-century in tone and imagery. The total darkness of death, like a ravenous wolf (perhaps a pun on the street-corner seducer), will assuredly reach the desired position of the lover. Agee's unconquerable vein

of melancholy lurks behind his sensual poetry like a
skull beneath a lover's mask.

In the second poem, the poet awakens one summer
noon from a bright dream of "plenitudes" and "fat
futurities" to the cruel and shadowy reality of daylight.
This daylight, dimmer than the brightness of the poet's
sleeping vision, is paradoxically both light and dark:

> The shade o'erswam me like a sheet
> Of draughty disappointed vans,
> And lobbered beak, and drawling feet.   (11)

Like Yeats's rough beast that slouches toward Bethlehem
to be born in "The Second Coming," this shade, both
shadow and spirit, with its draughty wings, lobbered beak,
and drawling feet, is a striking image, making this
otherwise commonplace poem memorable. Frustrated
dreams, incidentally, appear again later in "Description of
Elysium," the sixth poem in the volume. "Whole health
resides with peace" in this marvelous place, but, after an
enticing description, the poet concludes that "we can not
come there." Concerned with Elysium, Agee was
something of an escapist, always desiring a simpler world
but realizing that such a world exists only in dreams.
Reality, in Agee's verse, is always grim.

The frustration of love is again the theme of the third
lyric. All love spent, there is only pity for one another left
in this affair. Not one of Agee's best poems because of its
sentimentality, it is redeemed by a striking image at
the end:

> Feeling the cliff unmorsel from our heels
> And knowing balance gone, we smile, and stay
> A little, whirling our arms like desperate
>   wheels.   (12)

Frantically clawing for firm ground, these lovers find their
relationship slipping away bit by bit. The loneliness
arising from their desperate situation may account for
poems seven and ten. The seventh poem, a hymn to
creation, finds the poet one "shining night" "wandering
far alone" and weeping for wonder at the stars. Finding no
meaning in human relationships, the unhappy poet
searches for meaning in God's body. In the tenth poem,
the poet wears his heart on his sleeve again, weeps with
gladness, walks in the "brash brightening rain," and loiters
with his bride. The poems of a young man, the two lyrics
have all of the bad qualities of nineteenth-century
Romanticism. The poet falls upon the thorns of life and
bleeds, but he fails to find an "objective correlative" for his
emotion, a concrete embodiment in words for his
loneliness and despair.

There is a different attitude toward love, however, in the
ninth verse, "The Happy Hen," the only humorous poem
in the volume:

> His hottest love and most delight
> The rooster knows for speed of fear
> And winds her down and treads her right
> And leaves her stuffed with dazzled cheer,
>
> Rumpled allwhichways in her lint,
> Who swears, shrugs, redeems her face,
> And serves to mind us how a sprint
> Heads swiftliest for the state of grace.   (15)

Agee may have been reading D. H. Lawrence, for this
fable of rooster and hen reflects Lawrence's concern with
rapturous sexuality and uses one of Lawrence's main
symbols of virility—the cock. Chaucer also comes to mind.
Aside from such possible borrowings, the poem illustrates
human emotion through beastly action. Like females of

all species, the happy hen, after being "rumpled allwhichways in her lint," "swears, shrugs, redeems her face" and resigns herself to her role as procreator and the object of man's affection. In doing so, she achieves something like a "state of grace," implying that there is, despite the dictates of Behaviorism and Freudian psychology (the poem is ambiguously dedicated "to all scientific lovers"), something holy in the act regardless of how hotly it is performed.

The usual results of love are children, and poems four and five reveal Agee's concern with childhood. The fourth poem is about the death of a child, "this still folded leaf," that "fell fair in the fair season."

> Therefore with reason
> Dress all in cheer and lightly put away
>   With music and glad will
> This little child that cheated the long day
>   Of the long day's ill:
> Who knows this breathing joy, heavy on us all,
>   Never, never, never.   (12)

This simple and moving lyric achieves poignancy through paradox. Though having cheated the long day of the long day's ill, the child, no sooner blown than blasted, has also missed the "breathing [but heavy] joy" of life. The poet's attitude toward the child's death, therefore, is ambivalent. The fifth poem, entitled simply "A Song," is a variation on the same theme. The narrator of the lyric is the dead child's mother, and the poem is something of a macabre lullaby:

> Little child, take no fright,
> In that shadow where you are
> The toothless glowworm grants you light.
> Sure your mother's not afar.   (13)

The standard graveyard image of the worm as a "toothless glowworm," lighting the way to dusty death and granting light to the child's grave, lends this poem a chilling strangeness. The mother's comforting words console the child with the thought that soon she, too, like all of us, will be there with him. This grave is a fine and private place, but unlike so much Elizabethan verse which elaborates upon the same theme, it seems to have little religious meaning. Agee, a believing Christian, took his God seriously, but without sentimentality, and often with doubt. The eighth poem, for example, has an ominous tone and, because of images of thorn, holly, and nailed feet, a religious significance. But what Agee is saying is difficult to apprehend. Does the poem lament the loss of Christian values? It seems to, for the bare thorn rattling in the air and the footprint of a nailed foot in the sand suggest emptiness and desolation. *Permit Me Voyage* contains some excellent religious poetry, but many of Agee's most deeply felt poems seem confused and are of a questioning nature. Agee is constantly struggling toward belief, not expressing it. What is even more significant than Agee's belief or disbelief, however, is that, in this poem and in poem seven, he has worked in the dominant imagery of his major poem, "Ann Garner," thus providing the reader with another meaningful foreshadowing. *Light, dark, stars, silence,* and *snow* are significant words here, just as they are in the later poem. Like operatic *Leitmotifs,* the major images and ideas of the volume appear briefly in the opening ten lyrics and prepare the way for future usage.

It is only after the first ten poems, also, that Agee presents a "Dedication" to *Permit Me Voyage.* For readers accustomed to books dedicated "to my wife" or "to Helen," Agee's effort seems outrageous. Eight pages of dedication confront the wary reader, and names are

LIBRARY ST. MARY'S COLLEGE

cataloged with Whitmanesque verbosity. The dedication
begins

> in much humility
> to God in the highest
> in the trust that he despises nothing
>
> And in his commonwealth.

It is God's commonwealth that proves troublesome.
Everyone from Christ to Charlie Chaplin gains recognition
here, and Whitman, Hart Crane, Father Flye, Joyce,
Housman, Picasso, Einstein, and Toscanini are among
those to whom Agee is indebted. The book is also generally
dedicated to "those who know the high estate of art,
and who defend it" and to "the entire hierarchy of the
natural God, of every creature lone creator, in his truth
unthinkable, undimensionable, endlessness of endlessness:
beseeching him that he shall preserve this people."[12]
Since Agee's book is dedicated to all creators, it is fitting
that the final dedication be to God, the Supreme Creator:

> Have mercy upon us O great Lord God: for as there
> is some mercy, and the imagination of nobleness, even
> in this your creature, surely, surely there is mercy in
> you and honor and sweet might: and a way to hear,
> and a way to see, and wisdom, and careful love. Have
> mercy upon us therefore, O deep God of the void,
> spare this race in this your earth still in our free choice:
> who will turn to you, and again fail you, and once more
> turn as ever we have done. And make the eyes of our
> hearts, and the voice of our hearts in speech, honest
> and lovely within the fences of our nature, and a little
> clear.   (23)

The final statement, a plea for clarity, is a further clue to
Agee's mind: his wish as an artist was for clarity of

vision—"a way to see"—and clarity of speech. The
struggle toward perfect vision and honest speech was
Agee's concern all of his life, in spite of the fact that he
believed such perfection could never be achieved with
the written word.

"Ann Garner"

"Ann Garner" illustrates that not all of Agee's verse
was mere youthful outpouring. Narrative rather than
lyrical, this long poem of over three hundred lines is Agee's
most ambitious and most tightly controlled poetic
endeavor. Imagery of light, dark, silence, and snow link
the various sections of the work and enrich the texture.
Though much of the poem, as Agee himself described it, is
"simply iambic prose,"[13] many parts are lovely and the
story is skillfully told. Agee's descriptive touches,
reminiscent of van Gogh's fierce landscapes, are
particularly striking:

> The world rolled black and barren in its mists,
> And life was locked deep in the sheathing snows;
> Then wind and sun and rain came, like a lover,
> Clasping the world in fierce, caressing arms . . . (31)

>   All the heavens seemed to slip
> And swoop and shuttle, weaving a wild web
> Of gold across the sky. (33)

There is a Miltonic expansiveness in many of these lines,
a hint of dark and elemental forces shaping the universe,
and Agee's descriptions are compelling and frightening
at the same time.

The poem concerns Ann Garner, a farm wife who,
after giving birth to a stillborn child, becomes a symbol of
fertility to her neighbors and dies alone on a desolate

crest of pasture. Agee's theme is eternal recurrence, the
oneness of all nature, and the endless cycle of birth
and death. Ann, a fertility goddess, is big not only with
child but with the life force itself. She becomes one with
nature, "like a tree, or like the earth itself," and is looked
upon by the villagers as a sacred symbol:

> As long as Ann lived, all the countryside
> Was rich in produce—as long as Ann lived.   (32)

The villagers know, too, that

> She never could have died, save in some great
> Catastrophe of all the universe.   (32)

Ann's death, not a catastrophe but a triumph, comes as
she recognizes that there is a force that "sows the universe
anew." In a final scene that fuses life and death, Ann's
husband sprinkles the bones of her dead child into
her mouth and eyes, a symbolic ritual of husbandry, before
laying "the earth above her body." A framework on
which Agee could hang meditations about life and death,
"Ann Garner" reveals his true talent as a storyteller,
a talent he was later to develop more fully. The
Christian overtones of the story, in addition, are more
clear in "Ann Garner" than in Agee's other poems. Ann
has qualities of both Christ and the Virgin Mary.
Like Christ, she dies so that mankind will be saved. Her
fructifying energy will preserve humankind through
subsequent generations. On a mythological level, Ann
Garner is the deity who dies and is resurrected, thereby
assuring mankind that the crops will grow, the seasons will
continue their proper cycle, and the earth will forever
be fruitful. She is, too, like the Virgin in that she gives
miraculous birth to the life "locked deep in the sheathing

snows." None of Agee's themes is particularly new—that life and death are part of an eternal cycle is a theme appearing throughout literary history—but much of "Ann Garner" is redeemed by the poem's intensity, vivid imagery, and craftsmanship. If the poem fails in any way, it is due to Ann herself. The reader often fails to identify with Ann Garner, who, like all goddesses and deities, is distant, inexplicable, and strange. One could even argue that Ann is merely a bit deranged (she certainly has a Messianic complex); at any rate, she is beyond our mundane comprehension. Yet "Ann Garner," with its memorable story and lyric intensity, is Agee's finest poetical achievement.

"A Chorale" and "Epithalamium"

"A Chorale," like Agee's eighth lyric, is a poem lamenting the loss of Christian faith and values. Imploring Christ to awaken, the poet claims that men today "move in manners of their own devising" and "kill truth to find out truth more nearly," a man-made and not a God-made truth being the one they seek. The end of Christ's reign seems clearly in view to the poet:

> The time is withered of your ancient glory:
> Your doing in this sweet earth a pretty
>   story: (37)

In a request reminiscent of the great religious mystics, the poet asks God to "blaze in our hearts who still in earth commend you." This poem, struggling for clarity, again fails to particularize a spiritual loss of faith and fails to make the reader feel this loss. Juxtaposing the "ancient glory" of the Christian past with the "blind" present, Agee illuminates neither. His judgment of the present may be correct ("How knowledge muffles wisdom's eye

to danger:/How greed misrules . . .''), but his argument
is emotional and shrill. That other ages have been more
reverent than ours seems likely, but we have only the
poet's word for it. The poem, therefore, is indignant rather
than logically convincing.

"Epithalamium" is actually twelve poems, of varying
lengths, in praise of love. Still the work of a very young
man (Agee was twenty-one when he wrote this series of
poems), "Epithalamium" does not quite succeed.
There are two troubles here. "I'm very anxious not to
fall into archaism or 'literary' diction," he wrote in 1930.
"I want my vocabulary to have a very large range, but
the words *must* be alive."[14] Literary and archaic,
the diction of "Epithalamium" fails to live:

> For lo: from Oeta's wild and windflayed height
> A star takes wing, soars up the wide arched sky.   (38)

That "lo" and the reference to Oeta, indicative of the
poem in general, reveal a poet who had not yet discovered
a living idiom and a fresh vocabulary. Furthermore,
Agee's ego, sometimes enormous, creeps into the verse:

> For that he, in whose arms you soon shall lie,
> Not without guilt comes to a guiltless bride,
> Still fear him not, but tender at his side
> Recall his sorrow and his deep distress,
> Recall his loneliness.
>
> No boy has lived, but he has been his friend,
> No maiden but has lain within his arms.
> Hopeful of love fulfilled, he sought their charms,
> But all the visions that his full heart cherished
> In short time perished.   (39)

There is too much suffering in this solitary boy who
deliciously revels in his deep distress. "Epithalamium"

painfully reveals Agee's extreme youth, which, though not
in itself a deficit (Keats and Rimbaud come immediately
to mind), obstructs mature vision.

"Sonnets"

It is unnecessary to examine in detail all twenty-five
of Agee's sonnets. Some of them are mere exercises; others
are excellent achievements. All are skillful examples
of traditional sonneteering, and most follow the
octave-sestet division of the Shakespearean pattern. Like
Shakespeare, Agee is especially adept at forceful opening
lines: "I have been fashioned on a chain of flesh"
(Sonnet IV) and "Not of good will my mother's flesh was
wrought" (Sonnet XIV) are two striking examples. A
brief analysis of Sonnets I, XIV, and XXV will give
the reader some idea of the total work and perhaps tempt
him to read further. Sonnet I is an ideal fusion of theme
and form:

> So it begins. Adam is in his earth
> Tempted, and fallen, and his doom made sure
> O, in the very instant of his birth:
> Whose deathly nature must all things endure.
> The hungers of his flesh, and mind, and heart,
> That governed him when he was in the womb,
> These ravenings multiply in every part:
> And shall release him only to the tomb.
> Meantime he works the earth, and builds up nations,
> And trades, and wars, and learns, and worships
>   chance,
> And looks to God, and weaves the generations
> Which shall his many hungerings advance
> When he is sunken dead among his sins.
> Adam is in this earth. So it begins.   (46)

This circular poem, in good Elizabethan style, ends where
it begins, suggesting unity, order, and eternity. The
first and last lines form a chiasmus, linking above and
below, spirit and nature, Adam and his earth. Adam is in
the earth in two senses: he is buried there, and, being
all of us, he is still a part of it. Adam is clearly Everyman,
building up nations, appeasing the hungers of the
flesh, and worshiping chance. All of us, either through
original sin or mere human weakness, are Adams reborn,
succumbing to temptation and falling from God's
grace. The structure of the sonnet, too, suggests the
endless reenactment of Adam's temptation and fall. The
wearisome repetition of the word "and" throughout
the poem signifies the wearisome pace of Adam on this
earth.

Agee's sonnets, not without pattern, move from Adam,
through man in general, to the poet in particular.
Another pattern holding the work together is the theme
of questing. The sonnets can be viewed as an account
of the poet's quest for God. Sonnet XXV, the final one,
is the logical end of this quest. Here the poet concludes
that all earthly things are mutable—

> Be mindful, love, of love's mortality.
> Be mindful that all love is as the grass
> And all the goodliness of love the flower
> Of grass, for lo, its little day shall pass
> And withering and decay define its hour.
> All that we hold most lovely, and most cherish
> And most are proud in, all shall surely perish.   (49)

—and decides to "choose the course [his] fathers chose
before," to engage actively in life's struggle and to
seek unity in the chaos of human experience, to go
"mindless into truth." Sonnet XXV is a resolution to

"shut awhile" his "mouth that blabbed so loud with foreign song" until his throat can ring with the truth of God's creation and until the voice of his heart is truly honest (here we must recall that plea for clarity in the final lines of the "Dedication").

Sonnet XIV, concerning the poet's parents, is a perfect example of the clarity which Agee so earnestly sought. The poem achieves unity through images of husbandry:

> Not of good will my mother's flesh was wrought,
> Whose parents sowed in joy, and garnered care:
>
> The sullen harvest sudden winter brought
> Upon their time, outlasting their despair.
> Deep of a young girl's April strength his own
> My father's drank, and draughted her to age:
> Who in his strength met death and was outdone
> Of high and hopeless dreams, and grief, and rage.
>
> Poor wrath and rich humility, these met,
> Married, and sorrowing in a barren bed
> Their flesh embraced in pity did beget
> Flesh that must soon secure their fleshlihead:
> But knows not when, on whom cannot descry,
> And least of all could vaunt conjecture why.   (52)

The "sullen harvest" of this sowing yields barrenness, for all flesh—including the poet's—must come to dust. Man and wife beget "flesh that must soon secure their fleshlihead," a complex ambiguity. Fleshlihead can be seen simply as "flesh" with a suffix meaning state, condition, or character, and the poet implies that as his flesh grows, he makes secure and safe his parents' material state. Fleshlihead, like maidenhead, is also a kind of virginity, the body untouched by death or perhaps the body dead and untouched by impure life. "Fleshly head" seems also intended, implying that these parents are all too human. The poet suggests also that his flesh, like that of his parents, will soon find the grave. Rich in texture, this poem gathers complex meanings, subtly wrought, far beyond itself. Sowing and harvesting images link line to line, octet to sestet, making this one of Agee's best-constructed poems.

"Permit Me Voyage"

The final poem in the book is a fitting prayer entitled "Permit Me Voyage." The poet, his heart and mind all discharted and cast adrift in "this world of wildness," expresses a wish to be merely one "that shall preserve this race," a task difficult enough for anyone. "Permit me voyage, love, into your hands" is the poet's final plea to God. This poem, Sonnet XXV, and the final paragraph of the "Dedication" are a refutation of the belief that Agee might have become a greater poet had he not been lured by more commercial pursuits. On the contrary, Agee seems to have consciously abandoned poetry and its "foreign song." He clearly resolved to shut his "mouth that blabbed so loud." More specifically, he must have recognized that his poetry was the work of an extremely young man and that maturity was necessary for greater artistry. "One thing I feel is this," he wrote to Father Flye in 1932: "that a great deal of poetry is the product of adolescence—or of an emotionally adolescent frame of mind: and that as this state of mind changes, poetry is likely to dry up."[15] Perhaps he even realized that this drying up process had already begun to take place in him. At any rate, the decision to abandon poetry was both conscious and necessary.

Words, inadequate tools to begin with, are further limited by poetic form, meter, and rhyme. Agee

abandoned poetry not because of his inability, but because
of poetry's inability to do what he wanted it to do.
Confined by the limitations of the poetic line and its
accoutrements of meter, rhyme, and form, Agee turned
from poetry to modes of expression more suited to his
vision. His entire career, in fact, seems a search for
a manner of expression that would best enable him to see
his artistic creation as a living reality in the present
moment. Abandoning both poetry and prose, he
eventually found an ideal form, one that enables an artist
to create a world that exists solely in the present, that
captures—or, at least, can potentially capture—each
movement, detail, and nuance of physical reality: the
motion picture. But Agee's early talent was reportorial and
descriptive, and it was natural that after poetry he
would turn for adequate expression to reporting, as he
did in *Let Us Now Praise Famous Men.*

the failure
of reality

How was it we were caught?
—*Agee,* Let Us Now Praise Famous Men

      Let Us Now Praise Famous Men
is another Agee paradox. History, sociology, economics,
philosophy, and, in part, fiction, the book rejects all
attempts at easy classification and simple analysis. It is
appallingly overwritten, yet it is seldom boring. It has a
most unliterary subject, tenant farming in the South,
yet it contains some of the finest poetic prose in American
writing, poetry which Agee was unable to achieve in
Permit Me Voyage. Agee's attitude toward his subject is
idealized, sometimes almost mawkish, yet his writing
is always sincere and accurate. The student of literature
must resign himself to the fact that *Let Us Now Praise
Famous Men,* like *Moby Dick,* achieves greatness
through excess, paradox, and sheer linguistic power.

    It is with Melville's masterpiece that Agee's book most
clearly compares. Both works are written on an epic
scale in a rhetoric that is often ecstatic, sometimes
ponderous, and always awesome. Agee, says Alfred Kazin,
"had such an immense capacity for feeling and such easy
access to the rhetoric of English poetry that when not
taken in hand by his medium, he could oppress the

41

reader with merely beautiful words. His almost ecstatic feeling for music itself led him to seek unexpected dimensions in prose, and . . . to convey the feeling for the American land in highly charged rhythms that would stick close to the facts."[1] Like Melville, too, Agee had an awareness of the darker gods, a fascination for the abominations that dog man's footsteps to the grave. Agee's spectres were poverty and oppression, less overwhelming than Melville's whale but no less important, and his hatred of them gave the problem of tenant farming a universal quality and appeal.

American writing during the period of Agee's southern journey seemed, as Kazin states in *On Native Grounds,* "to impose new obligations." Writers, no longer expressing personality, expressed "belief, a participation at once so urgent and so vague that unusual sensibility seemed almost immoral in a world where mediocrity could conceal itself by the assumption of a political faith that compensated for the lack of perceptions by decrying the need of them. . . . Armed with a political concept, the writer felt that his 'realism' had a new foundation and literature itself a new dimension; and if what he produced was not always literature, his militancy augured a finer and riper humanity."[2] To see Agee as just another writer on the Left, however, is to misrepresent him, for he was an artist and not a propagandist. An armchair anarchist, as Agee called himself, he was a writer of perception as well as political faith and his aim was to produce works of art. That his artistic vision was heightened by the atmosphere of the Left was, if not accidental, certainly advantageous. "The strongest writers of the thirties," Daniel Aaron has pointed out, "used politics and were not used by it."[3]

Once in the South as a "spy" for *Fortune,* Agee became obsessed with his subject and worked, according to his companion Walker Evans, in "a rush and a rage.

In Alabama he was possessed with the business, jamming
it all into the days and the nights. He must not have
slept."[4] Ultimately, the articles from this southern
journey were never printed. Angry, exuberant, stylistically
avant-garde, such writing was certainly not the thing
for readers of *Fortune* or for armchair liberals who
wished to feel pity and not guilt. Agee finally decided to
put what he saw and felt in Alabama into a book,
and finished the manuscript on a farm in Frenchtown,
New Jersey. Richard Oulahan tells the story of the
genesis of the book:

> Agee's painstaking carving of every word into stone
> is recalled by Father Flye, who once spent a weekend
> on a New Jersey farm with the author and his family
> when he was finishing *Let Us Now Praise Famous Men*.
> Agee had worked for three years and had written 300,000
> words, more than twice the length of the published
> book. For years he had felt that "the tenant book," as
> he called it, was a botch. He had tried, at first, to write
> it on the level of the tenant farmers themselves, so they
> could understand it. "I made a try," he wrote Father
> Flye. "I felt it was a failure. The lives of these families
> belong . . . to people like them. . . . The least I can do
> is return the property where it belongs." But writing on
> a sharecropper's level would not work, and Agee reverted
> to his own style. "If you're going to write what may
> be poison," he told the priest, "better write it to adults
> than to perfectly defenseless children."
>
> On the weekend Agee was at last finishing the book,
> Father Flye and Agee's family kept a discreet distance
> until the author emerged from his study. "Well, it's
> done," he said. "Now we'll take it to the publisher."
> Everyone got into the family car, with the finished
> manuscript, and started toward New York. Halfway
> to Lincoln Tunnel, Agee suddenly stopped. "Oh, no,"

he said. "I've just had another idea on how to do a whole
section over again." So they made a U-turn back to New
Jersey, and the book was finally published two years later.[5]

The book was received well by critics when it came out
in 1941 but failed to catch on with the public. Within
a short while it was remaindered and then put out of print.

Let Us Now Praise Famous Men is a study of three
Alabama tenant families: The Woodses, the Rickettses,
and the Gudgers. The book was intended to be the
first volume of a larger work which would have been
called *Three Tenant Families.* Agee never got beyond the
first volume, a testimony to the difficulty he faced. His
problem, as he fully realized, was to recreate the lives of
the tenant families without pity or shame, to make the
reader live their problems and share the guilt for
their predicament. The book, Agee explained in his
preface, is an "effort to recognize the stature of a portion
of unimagined existence, and to contrive techniques
proper to its recording, communication, analysis, and
defense. More essentially, this is an independent inquiry
into certain normal predicaments of human divinity."[6]

In order to understand fully what Agee was trying to
do in *Let Us Now Praise Famous Men,* one must first
understand the nature of literary social protest. Too
often the protest writer sees his problem as a horror that
needs only to be cataloged and recognized in order to be
alleviated or abolished by the existing social framework.
The common attitude of the protest writer is "This
is horrible," and the corresponding attitude of the reader
is one of sympathy, pity, and disgust. "The 'protest' novel,"
points out James Baldwin, "so far from being disturbing,
is an accepted and comforting aspect of the American
scene, ramifying that framework we believe to be so
necessary. Whatever unsettling questions are raised are
evanescent, titillating; remote, for this has nothing to do

with us, it is safely ensconced in the social arena, where, indeed, it has nothing to do with anyone, so that finally we receive a very definite thrill of virtue from the fact that we are reading such a book at all. This report from the pit reassures us of its reality and its darkness and of our own salvation."[7] It was precisely this "thrill of virtue" that Agee was trying to avoid. He was convinced, as Lionel Trilling states, that "Christian pity is not enough. Liberal concern and good will are hopeless; lack of passion is here an insult."[8]

Agee's task, then, was to write about the Woodses, the Rickettses, and the Gudgers as human beings and not as social problems, to avoid all attitudes of middle-class pity and superiority, and to filter his experience through a clarifying consciousness, one with roots in the prosperous middle class and with liberal and Christian attitudes. The question he had to pursue, as Trilling points out, was "How may we—'we' being the relatively fortunate middle class that reads books and experiences emotions—how may we feel about the—and the word itself proclaims the difficulty—under-privileged?"[9] In order to answer this question honestly, Agee chose to use himself as the central consciousness. Throughout the book one is constantly aware of Agee's analyzing his attitudes toward these Alabama farmers, always asking himself, "How much of my present emotion is hypocritical?"

Furthermore, Agee was hindered by the fact that he, unlike the fiction writer, had to work solely within the confines of reality. He states this clearly in an early part of the book:

> In a novel, a house or person has his meaning, his existence, entirely through the writer. Here, a house or a person has only the most limited of his meaning through me; his true meaning is much huger. It is that he *exists,* in actual being, as you do and as I do, and as no character of

the imagination can possibly exist. His great weight,
mystery, and dignity are in this fact. As for me, I can
tell you of him only what I saw, only so accurately as in
my terms I know how: and this in turn has its chief stature
not in any ability of mine but in the fact that I too exist,
not as a work of fiction, but as a human being. Because
of his immeasurable weight in actual existence, and because
of mine, every word I tell of him has inevitably a kind
of immediacy, a kind of meaning, not at all necessarily
"superior" to that of imagination, but of a kind so different
that a work of the imagination (however intensely it may
draw on "life") can at best only faintly imitate the
least of it.[10]

The fiction writer, sole creator of his world, faces no such
problem as Agee faced here. Restricted entirely to the
accurate representation of real people and events, Agee
intended his study of cotton tenantry to be "exhaustive,
with no detail, however trivial it may seem, left untouched,
no relevancy avoided, which lies within the power of
remembrance to maintain, of the intelligence to perceive,
and of the spirit to persist in."[11] Long chapters are
devoted to money, shelter, clothing, education, and work,
chapters which many readers might find tedious. In
the Whitman tradition, Agee itemizes each detail of his
subjects' daily life, a means of expression designed
to place the reader squarely within the tenant farmers'
world and to force the reader to focus his sensibility from
within the framework of the material.

Words, inadequate tools at best, are supplemented by
the photographs of Walker Evans. The text and the
photographs are, according to Agee, "coequal, mutually
independent, and fully collaborative."[12] Reacting against
the pseudo-realistic photography of Margaret Bourke-
White and Paul Strand and the equally unreal realism of
the regional painting of Grant Wood and Thomas Hart

Benton, Evans envisioned his photographs as family
snapshots, giving them an immediacy unattained by the
false seriousness of "artistic" photography. Lionel
Trilling, reviewing the book in 1941, found that the
beauty of Evans' work lay in "its perfect taste, taking that
word in its largest possible sense to mean tact, delicacy,
justness of feeling, complete awareness and perfect
respect. It is a tremendously impressive moral quality."[13]
All of Evans' subjects are posed, self-consciously facing
the naked eye of the camera, and are captured forever,
like Greek statues, in moments of fear, pride, and
suffering. The photograph of Mrs. Gudger, which Trilling
called "one of the finest objects of any art of our time."[14]
and the one of Mrs. Ricketts have a quality of
suffering and dignity which few paintings and no other
photographs of our time reveal.

Agee, through the poverty of mere written words, had
to match the stunning impact of these photographs.
"If I could do it, I'd do no writing at all here," Agee
admitted. "It would be photographs; the rest would
be fragments of cloth, bits of cotton, lumps of earth,
records of speech, pieces of wood and iron, phials of
odors, plates of food and of excrement."[15] Eschewing both
journalism, "a broad and successful form of lying,"[16]
and "art," which by its very nature alters reality, Agee
conceived his text as a way of seeing, a means of writing
"of nothing whatever which did not in physical actuality
or in the mind happen or appear," and resolved "not to
use these 'materials' for art, far less for journalism,
but *to give them as they were and as in my memory and
regard they are*."[17] What he wanted to do, Agee
concluded, was "to tell this as exactly and clearly as I
can and get the damned thing done with."[18]

The structure of the book, much maligned by critics
and readers, is a problem, but not an insurmountable one.
It is not that the book is devoid of structure. On the

contrary, it has several structures. One consists of
four planes:

> That of recall; of reception, contemplation, *in medias
> res;* for which I have set up this silence under darkness
> on this front porch as a sort of fore-stage to which from
> time to time the action may have occasion to return.
>
> "As it happened": the straight narrative at the prow as
> from the first to last day it cut unknown water.
>
> By recall and memory from the present: which is a part
> of the experience: and this includes imagination, which in
> the other planes I swear myself against.
>
> As I try to write it: problems of recording; which, too,
> are an organic part of the experience as a whole.[19]

These four planes might also be described as flashback,
chronological narrative, imaginative reconstruction, and
central consciousness. The device of flashback allowed
Agee to contemplate and recall the events that led up
to the present moment, while chronological narrative
presented events in their logical time sequence.
Imaginative reconstruction differed from flashback in
that the former was free to invent, to fictionally recreate in
order to gain complete perspective. Finally, central
consciousness was the detailed account of the perceiving
mind of the artist. Agee used each of these methods,
and each provided him with a vantage point from which to
record.

A second structure might best be seen in terms of
music. The book has a pattern, much like the sonata form,
consisting of two major themes, both of which are
stated in the opening pages:

> Poor naked wretches, whereso'er you are,
> That bide the pelting of this pitiless storm.

How shall your houseless heads and unfed sides,
Your loop'd and window'd raggedness, defend you
From seasons such as these? O! I have ta'en
Too little care of this! Take physic, pomp;
Expose thyself to feel what wretches feel,
That thou may'st shake the superflux to them,
And show, the heavens are just.   [*King Lear,*
III, iv, 28-36]

The second theme is "Workers of the world, unite and fight. You have nothing to lose but your chains, and a world to win."[20] The initial theme—poverty—dominates this symphonic structure, while the second, injustice, appears as a subdominant theme. Better still, the entire work is a set of variations or a *grosse fugue* on the theme of poverty and human suffering.

Still a third structure can be found in the dramatic form of the book, especially in the sections titled "On the Porch." It is likely that Agee conceived *Let Us Now Praise Famous Men,* on one level, as drama. There is one section called "Intermission: Conversation in the Lobby"; and the book divides into three parts, which correspond to the three acts of a play.[21] Agee even provides, in the opening pages, a cast of characters. Reminiscent of the opening pages of *A Death in the Family,* the sections titled "On the Porch" serve to set the scene for the human drama being unfolded:

The house and all that was in it had now descended deep beneath the gradual spiral it had sunk through; it lay formal under the order of entire silence. In the square pine room at the back the bodies of the man of thirty and of his wife and of their children lay on shallow mattresses on their iron beds and on the rigid floor, and they were sleeping, and the dog lay asleep in the hallway.

Most human beings, most animals and birds who live
in the sheltering ring of human influence, and a great
portion of all the branched tribes of living in earth and
air and water upon a half of the world, were stunned
with sleep. That region of the earth on which we were at
this time transient was some hours fallen beneath the
fascination of the stone, steady shadow of the planet, and
lay now listing toward the last depth; and
now by a blockade of the sun were clearly disclosed
those discharges of light which teach us what little we
can learn of the stars and of the true nature of our
surroundings.[22]

It is as if the narrator, and the reader with him, are
sinking level by level into that state of semi-consciousness,
halfway between sleep and wakefulness, which so often
brings up memories from the labyrinth of the human
mind. There is a somnambulistic rhythm to Agee's prose
and a feeling of the closeness of the entire universe,
as if all the suffering and misery of the world were
concentrated in this microcosm. Beginning with sleep, the
book ends the same way, thus making it circular,
complete and organic: "Our talk drained rather quickly
off into silence and we lay thinking, analyzing,
remembering, in the human and artist's sense praying,
chiefly over matters of the present and of that immediate
past which was a part of the present; and each of these
matters had in that time the extreme clearness, and edge,
and honor, which I shall now try to give you; until
at length we too fell asleep."[23] Too often, however, as
Agee continually reminds us, this dream world becomes
a nightmare, in which archetypal patterns of misery and
human dignity in the face of suffering come to the fore.

   Let Us Now Praise Famous Men, concerned with "the
cruel radiance of what is,"[24] contains many memorable

sections. There is the scene with the three young Negro
singers ("summoned to sing for Walker and for me,"
says Agee, "to show us what nigger music is like"[25]),
which contains one of the finest descriptions in the English
language of the shape and sound of music:

> They ran in a long and slow motion and convolution of
> rolling as at the bottom of a stormy sea, voice meeting
> voice as ships in dream, retreated, met once more, much
> woven, digressions and returns of time, quite tuneless, the
> bass, over and over, approaching, drooping, the same
> declivity, the baritone taking over, a sort of metacenter,
> murmuring along monotones between major and minor,
> nor in any determinable key, the tenor winding upward
> like a horn, a wire, the flight of a bird, almost into full
> declamation, then failing it, silencing; at length enlarging,
> the others lifting, now, alone, lone, and largely, questioning,
> alone and not sustained, in the middle of space, stopped;
> and now resumed, sunken upon the bosom of the bass,
> the head declined; both muted, droned; the baritone
> makes his comment, unresolved, that is a question, all
> on one note: and they are quiet, and do not look at us,
> nor at anything.[26]

The scene with the young Negro couple, frightened by
Agee on a country road, stands out, too, as does Agee's
first night with the Gudger family and his battle with
their bedbugs and lice.

In contrast to these realistic scenes, the poetic
passages, "On the Porch," "All over Alabama," and
"Colon," serve to balance and break up the long sections
of detail, making the book a dialogue of fact and fancy,
spirit and substance, body and soul. The poetry in
these passages is the work of a mature poet, one who no
longer relies on archaic poetic diction and "prettying up"

for his effects as did the young Agee of *Permit Me Voyage*. As Dwight Macdonald has said, Agee's best poetry "is written in prose and is buried in his three books."[27]

Lying behind the beauty and poetry of this book, however, is a bitter social criticism, a barely restrained anger at all those whose complacency and cruelty "in so immane and outrageous, wild, irresponsible, dangerous-idiot a world"[28] extinguishes the godhead in the heart, nerves, and center of other human lives. Running throughout the book, explicitly and implicitly, is this theme:

> In what way were we trapped? where, our mistake?
> what, where, how, when, what way, might all these things
> have been different, if only we had done otherwise? if
> only we might have known. Where lost that bright health
> of love that knew so surely it would stay; how, how did
> it sink away, beyond help, beyond hope, beyond desire,
> beyond remembrance; and where the weight and the
> wealth of that strong year when there was more to eat than
> we could hold, new clothes, a grafanola, and money in
> the bank? How, how did all this sink so swift away, like
> that grand august cloud who gathers—the day quiets dark
> and chills, and the leaves lather—and scarcely steams
> the land? How are these things?[29]

Each human being contributes to the misery of his fellow man, through either cruelty or indifference, and the suffering of the tenant farmers is due not so much to the savageness of the world, according to Agee, as to the shirking "of the true weight of responsibility which each human being must learn to undertake for all others."[30]

Along with Thoreau, the Naturalists, the Muckrakers, and the protest novelists of the thirties, Agee is squarely in the mainstream of American liberal writers. Agee's

ironic quotations from a third-grade geography textbook
belonging to one of the Gudger children is both a bitter
indictment of education and a painful emphasis of the
Gudgers' true condition: "Let us imagine that we are far
out in the fields. The air is bitter cold and the wind is
blowing. Snow is falling, and by and by it will turn into
sleet and rain. We are almost naked. We have nothing
to eat and are suffering from hunger as well as cold.
Suddenly the Queen of the Fairies floats down and offers
us three wishes."[31] There is no Queen of the Fairies
for these children who "live in a steady shame and insult
of discomforts, insecurities, and inferiorities, piecing
these together into whatever semblance of comfortable
living they can."[32] To free the minds of these tenant
children, however, would be equally a disaster. The best
that has been thought and said in the world has little
practical value for a child who will inevitably spend his
life growing someone else's cotton. Many of them were
beyond help from the very beginning of their lives: their
intellects "died before they were born; they hang behind
their eyes like fetuses in alcohol."[33] The failure of
education to deal realistically with these tenant children
is a major part of the world's failure—ours—to alleviate
misery and poverty. Agee's criticism of American
education and society is as caustic as Upton Sinclair's
exposure of the Chicago stockyards, Sinclair Lewis'
denunciation of Main Street, and John Dos Passos'
arraignment of capitalism. One of the outstanding social
documents of the socially conscious thirties, *Let Us
Now Praise Famous Men* ranks equally high in the entire
field of American protest writing.

Despite the fact that *Let Us Now Praise Famous Men*
is, as Lionel Trilling claims, "a great book,"[34] it is
flawed in two important ways. The first flaw is a moral
one, the second is artistic. Trilling, in his 1941 review,

pointed out that Agee's was "a failure of moral realism" that lay in his "inability to see these people as anything but good."[35] "Not that he falsified what is apparent," continued Trilling: "for example he can note with perfect directness their hatred of Negroes; and not that he is ever pious or sentimental, like Steinbeck and Hemingway. But he writes of his people as if there were no human unregenerateness in them, no flicker of malice or meanness, no darkness or wildness of feeling, only a sure and simple virtue, the growth, we must suppose, of their hard, unlovely poverty."[36] Essentially correct, Trilling misses part of the point. Agee, attempting to record experience through his own consciousness, is recording *his* attitudes, not inherent qualities of the tenant farmers. There is no malice or meanness in these people because Agee came to see them as noble human beings, almost folk-heroes, as "famous men." Surely Agee is not saying that there is no malice or darkness in these human souls; he is, however, saying that through suffering comes nobility and that everything that is, even the dirty, barefoot child of a tenant family, is holy. It is not so much tenant farmers as humankind that concerns Agee here, and the Gudgers, Rickettses, and Woodses are a microcosm of the macrocosm. Agee's vision is essentially positive and religious (which is something other than Christian, though his vision is that, too): "In every child who is born, under no matter what circumstances, and of no matter what parents, the potentiality of the human race is born again: and in him too, once more, and of each of us, our terrific responsibility towards human life; towards the utmost idea of goodness, of the horror of error, and of God."[37] The sure and simple virtue that Agee saw in the tenant families of Alabama was the same virtue he saw in mankind. Man will prevail, for through suffering he finds strength. Trilling's accusation, therefore, that Agee's was

a "failure of moral realism," the liberal idealist's too
frequent failure to see his socially deprived subject as
anything other than virtuous, does not seem correct. It has
been common for American social reformers to be deceived
by what Richard Hofstadter, in *The Age of Reform,* has
called "the folklore of Populism."[38] Richard Chase sees
this folklore as having two origins:

> First, there is what Mr. Hofstadter calls the "agrarian
> myth" that ever since the time of Jefferson has haunted
> the mind, not of the vast commercialized middle class or
> perhaps after the earliest times the farmers either, but of
> reformers and intellectuals. This "myth" involves the idea
> of a pastoral golden age—a time of plain living,
> independence, self-sufficiency and closeness to the soil—an
> idea which has been celebrated in various ways by
> innumerable American writers. Second, there is the
> mythology of Calvinism which especially in the rural West
> and South has always infused Protestantism, even the
> non-Calvinist sects, with its particular kind of Manichaean
> demonology.[39]

It is this "agrarian myth" that Trilling possibly has in
mind. There is no reason, however, to think that Agee did
not know what he was doing. I think it is more accurate,
then, to see Agee's vision in *Let Us Now Praise Famous
Men* as a consciously restricted point of view rather
than a failure.

Agee's second error was an artistic one. Although, as
I pointed out, there are several structures in *Let Us Now
Praise Famous Men,* the book still lacks unity and
discipline. The structures are general, and what one misses
is the shaping hand of the skillful artist. The book, like
an oversized suit, hangs loose in several places.
Reminiscent of Thomas Wolfe's novels, it is exuberant,

full of wild energy and fury, and sometimes willfully devoid of discipline. "Without any qualification and if necessary with belligerence," Agee said, "I respect and believe in even the most supposedly 'fantastic' works of the imagination."[40] But he also said once that the "roots are emotion and intuitiveness; the chief necessity is discipline."[41] Agee was, I believe, caught between these two notions. And, finally, I think he was led astray by the deleterious effect of Naturalist writing. "Who cares for fine style!" Frank Norris said in a letter to Isaac Marcosson. "Tell your yarn and let your style go to the devil. We don't want literature, we want life."[42] Agee reminds us, like Norris, that he is not trying to write "art." "Calling for the moment everything except art Nature," he states, "I would insist that everything in Nature, every most casual thing, has an inevitability and perfection which art as such can only approach, and shares in fact, not as art, but as the part of Nature that it is; so that, for instance, a contour map is at least as considerably an image of absolute 'beauty' as the counterpoints of Bach which it happens to resemble."[43] This theory, that art is a kind of second-class Nature and that every part of Nature contains absolute beauty, is unconvincing. If it is true, why bother to create art at all? Why not relax and enjoy the "absolute beauty" of a contour map, a sunset, or—for that matter— a tenant farmer? Agee's insistence that the things of this world have an absolute beauty of their own and need no assistance from art betrays him into a shameless lack of responsibility in his use of language.

Agee's "failure" might better be termed a failure of reality, the failure of the real to be as interesting, inevitable, and perfect as fiction. Malcolm Cowley says in *The Literary Situation:*

I have always felt by instinct that language was the central problem of any writer, in any creative medium. If he

lacks the sense of words he may be an admirable scholar,
a moral philosopher, a student of human behavior, or a
contriver of big dramatic scenes, but he isn't properly
a writer. Yeats said that style in literature is what
corresponds to the moral element in men of action. I
think he meant that style is the result of an infinite
number of choices, all determined by standards of what is
linguistically right and wrong. "Books live almost entirely
because of their style," he said—and he was echoing a
long line of creative artists who felt that until the right
words have been found for an action it does not exist in
words, in literature.[44]

Agee, I suspect, eventually came to realize his mistaken
judgment when writing *Let Us Now Praise Famous Men*
and, for that reason, soon turned to fiction. It is only there,
he must have seen, that the "truth" that comes from
artistic discipline and from finding the right words in the
right order, for example, the truth that is revealed in
A Death in the Family, shines forth.

   If Agee's book fails, it fails—like so many other
books in American literature—in the grand manner.
Let Us Now Praise Famous Men, despite its flaws, failures,
and excesses, is an outstanding document in American
writing, and is best summed up, I think, by Dwight
Macdonald:

[*Let Us Now Praise Famous Men* is] a young man's
book—exuberant, angry, tender, willful to the point of
perversity (for example, the clumsy and undescriptive
title), with the most amazing variations in quality; most
of it is extremely good, some of it is as great prose as
we have had since Hawthorne, and some of it is turgid,
mawkish, overwritten; discriminating cuts would have
enormously improved the book. But the author gives
himself wholly to his theme and brings to bear all his

powers; he will go to any lengths to get it just right. From this emerges a truth that includes and goes beyond the truth about poverty and ignorance in sociological studies (and "realistic" novels), the truth that such squalid lives, imaginatively observed, are also touched with the poetry, the comedy, the drama of what is unexpected and unpredictable because it is living.[45]

But Agee did not "get it just right." The artistry that he was to achieve through discipline was yet to come. In the last years of his life, he attained a firmer control over his material and a more mature vision, and this synthesis of technique, control, and imagination that changes a "writer" into an "artist" is found mainly in Agee's fiction.

the truth
of fiction

iv

*Underlying the hopefulness is utter
lack of confidence, apathy, panic
and despair.*
—*Agee,* Letters to Father Flye

Art must, Joseph Conrad claimed
in his famous preface to *The Nigger of the "Narcissus,"*

strenuously aspire to the plasticity of sculpture, to the
colour of painting, and to the magic suggestiveness of
music—which is the art of arts. And it is only through
complete, unswerving devotion to the perfect blending of
form and substance; it is only through unremitting
never-discouraged care for the shape and ring of sentences
that an approach can be made to plasticity, to colour,
and that the light of magic suggestiveness may be brought
to play for an evanescent instant over the commonplace
surface of words: of the old, old words, worn thin,
defaced by ages of careless usage.[1]

"My task which I am trying to achieve is," Conrad
continued, "by the power of the written word, to make you
hear, to make you feel—it is, before all, to make you *see*."[2]
These statements could easily have come from James Agee.
Although his prose never reached the symbolic and
evocative level of Conrad's in *Heart of Darkness* or

Victory, Agee did aspire to more than just literal realism—
in, for example, *The Morning Watch* and *A Death in the
Family.* Like Conrad, Agee attempted to capture and
reproduce in prose each fleeting moment of human
existence, to create prose fiction with "the magic
suggestiveness of music," to produce, as Henry James
once said, "the illusion of life."[3] Again like Conrad, Agee
struggled—some say unsuccessfully—to blend form and
substance in perfect proportions.

Just as Agee was always a poet, so was he always a
film scenarist. His vision was constantly in terms of the
photograph, the motion picture, and the camera lens. His
descriptive technique is that of the slow-motion camera
which captures each nuance of color, shading, and light
and seems to hold it for just a second in an eternal present.
Knoxville, for example, in *A Death in the Family,* opens
up, page by page, like a slow-motion film of a blooming
flower:

> Waking in darkness, he saw the window. Curtains, a tall,
> cloven wave, towered almost to the floor. Transparent,
> manifold, scalloped along their inward edges like the
> valves of a sea creature, they moved delectably on the air
> of the open window.
> Where they were touched by the carbon light of the
> street lamp, they were as white as sugar. The extravagant
> foliage which had been wrought into them by machinery
> showed even more sharply white where the light touched,
> and elsewhere was black in the limp cloth.
> The light put the shadows of moving leaves against the
> curtains, which moved with the moving curtains and upon
> the bare glass between the curtains.
> Where the light touched the leaves they seemed to burn,
> a bitter green. Elsewhere they were darkest gray and
> darker. Beneath each of these thousands of closely

assembled leaves dwelt either no natural light or richest darkness. Without touching each other these leaves were stirred as, silently, the whole tree moved in its sleep.

Directly opposite his window was another. Behind this open window, too, were curtains which moved and against them moved the scattered shadows of other leaves. Beyond these curtains and beyond the bare glass between, the room was as dark as his own.

He heard the summer night.[4]

This evocative description pans from bedroom to window to opposite window, lingering for a close-up of the bedroom window touched by the shadows of moving leaves and illuminated by the carbon light of a street lamp. Agee's description, a motion-picture in words, is worthy of an imaginative film director who sees his setting in terms of light, darkness, mood, and movement, and captures it in a sweeping shot which carries the viewer from the confines of a darkened bedroom to the summer night beyond.

It was precisely because of his attempt to reproduce in words a cinematic vision of experience that James Agee turned to fiction. Poetry, with its necessities of conciseness, rhythm, and control, was too limited a medium to reproduce this vision, to represent the interplay of human personalities in a faithfully realistic setting. Reportage was restricted to the details of reality; it left no room for the creative imagination. Only in fiction could Agee paradoxically find the necessary discipline and freedom that his artistry required. Only in fiction could Agee find all of those qualities which give a work of fiction the semblance of actuality and, at the same time, make it into something more, that which we distinguish as "art." And fiction, too, made fewer disciplinary demands upon an author like Agee, whose prose often slipped its confines and galloped off uncontrollably.

Agee's Shorter Fiction

At the present time, any study of Agee's fiction must necessarily be incomplete. There are, we are told by those who knew him, short stories—possibly novels—yet unpublished.[5] The shorter fiction that we now have is slight. Aside from *A Death in the Family* and the novella *The Morning Watch,* there remains only one short story, "A Mother's Tale," and a *Fortune* article, "Six Days at Sea," capable of standing as finished artistic achievements. Much of Agee's magnificent prose is buried in anonymous and ephemeral articles for commercial magazines: stories about weaving and gambling, a fine report of postwar Europe, the *Time* magazine accounts of President Roosevelt's death and the bombing of Hiroshima.

Although the product of a reportorial assignment, "Six Days at Sea" deserves study as a short story. It has all the qualifications: artistic unity, masterful prose, character analysis, and meaningful statement. Published in *Fortune* magazine along with photographs by Walker Evans, this story, outwardly concerned with the T.E.L. (turbo-electric liner) *Oriente* bound for Havana, Cuba, is a thinly disguised account of middle-class values, morals, and customs. Unlike the rest of Agee's prose works, firmly grounded in humanism and compassion, this story is a bitter attack, full of rapier thrusts, delicate carvings, and brutal axe-blows. It was, as Agee himself must have realized, a rare opportunity *épater les bourgeois.*

We are told, beneath the title of the article, that "Fortune sent an anonymous reporter on a cruise, and he came back with this human document that has little to do with the profound economic problems of the merchant marine" (this issue of *Fortune* was entirely devoted to such "profound" problems).[6] The statement sounds delightfully tongue-in-cheek, although one could safely bet, knowing

Fortune, that it was meant to be taken seriously. Perhaps
tacked on to appease the predictable indignation of their
readers, the statement seems contradicted by the story that
follows it. This is no mere "human document" (a phrase
smacking of togetherness, Norman Rockwell magazine
covers, and the *Reader's Digest*), nor is this just another
"anonymous reporter." Agee, from the very opening,
reveals himself as an artist with a poet's eye for detail:
"The sun stood bright on the clean, already warm decks,
the blue water enlarged without whitening, and sang
along the flanks of the ship like seltzer."[7] More memorable
than the descriptions are the caustic character portraits on
this ship of fools: "A blond young man who resembled
an airedale sufficiently intelligent to count to ten, dance fox
trots, and graduate from a gentleman's university came
briskly to the dining room in sharply pressed slacks and a
navy blue sports shirt, read the sign, dashed away, and
soon reappeared plus a checkered coat and a plaid tie."[8]
Like the young "airedales" who parade about the deck in
"naughty bathing trunks," leisurely smack tennis balls
back and forth to one another, and furiously search for
sexual adventures, the other passengers are similar
"representatives of the lower to middle brackets of the
American urban middle class."[9] Agee typifies them in a
passage worthy of Sinclair Lewis or H. L. Mencken at
their best:

> They were of that vast race whose freedom falls in
> summer and is short. Leisure, being no part of their
> natural lives, was precious to them; and they were aboard
> this ship because they were convinced that this was going
> to be as pleasurable a way of spending that leisure as
> they could afford or imagine. What they made of it, of
> course, and what they failed to make, they made in a
> beautifully logical image of themselves: of their lifelong

environment, of their social and economic class, of their
mothers, of their civilization. And that includes their
strongest and most sorrowful trait: their talent for
self-deceit.[10]

We find here, as in a medieval woodcut, an assortment
of universal types: the rich Jewess, the "roguish fellow of
forty," the homely wallflower, the college boy, the urbane
headwaiter ("a prim Arthur Treacher type"), the unhappy
married couple. All are minor characters in this serio-comic
voyage which becomes symbolic of more than a simple
passage to Havana.

Agee's satire is unmerciful, and it is wickedly funny.
Agee creates a Swiftian world of frustrated Lilliputians
and occasional Brobdingnagians, all leading lives of quiet
desperation. Take, for example, the belle of the *Oriente*
ball:

> The wow of the evening was a blonde who was born out
> of her time: her glad and perpetually surprised face was
> that which appears in eighteenth century pornographic
> engravings wherein the chore boy tumbles the milkmaid
> in an explosion of hens and alfalfa. Her dress was cut
> with considerable extra *élan* to set off her uncommonly
> beautiful breasts, which in the more extreme centrifuges
> of the dance swung almost entirely free of ambush. She
> had a howling rush and a grand time. The six Cuban
> boys watched her constantly and chattered among
> themselves. Whenever she approached their corner their
> plum-jelly eyes bugged out with love. Twice, without a
> trace of anything save naïve admiration too great to be
> restrained, they broke into applause.[11]

This buxom creature, straight from a Hogarth engraving,
is not believable, nor is she meant to be. She is emblematic

of desirable and slightly wicked femininity, and Agee has
described her in an eternal pose, beguiling, voluptuous,
and elusive, while the six Cuban boys, making no rake's
progress, ogle her with admiration.

Not everyone on this cruise, however, has "a howling
rush and a grand time." After a few middle-class days in
Havana ("The music was every bit as smooth as Wayne
King and even the native Cubans . . . seemed an awfully
nice, refined class of people"), these fabulous voyagers
sadly depart while "men and boys dive for coins in the foul
olive water."[12] The return trip becomes a nightmare:
"Inhibitions began to drop off like clothes at a Norman
Rockwell swimming hole. Several of the girls to whom a
good time meant most and who were in that proportion the
most cruelly disappointed members of the cruise, began to
get pretty drunk and pretty loud."[13] The tone of the return
is remarkably captured in one dramatic vignette, which
spotlights the essential meanness of these lives: "A wife
and husband sat in a dark corner talking intensely: two
phrases kept re-emerging with almost liturgical monotony:
k e e p   y o u r   v o i c e   d o w n,   a n d   g o d   d a m n   y o u.
A n d   g o d   d a m n   y o u   t o o   y o u   g o d   d a m n e d.
Quite suddenly she struck her full glass of planter's punch
into his lap and they left the table walking stiffly, their
whole bodies fists."[14]

What clearly emerges in this journalistic effort is
Agee's increasing awareness of the craft of fiction. What
could have been merely one more slick article turns out
to be, in both quality and technique, a short story. We find,
in "Six Days at Sea," a coherent plot structure with a
conflict between an initial purpose (the quest for a
hedonistic Utopia) and the ultimate failure of that purpose
(the cruel fact of mundane reality). Within this broad
pattern, Agee has woven a variety of characters whose
purposes interconnect. The texture of the work reveals a

beautifully controlled irony throughout the story, and the story's resolution, shown in vignettes like that of the quarreling couple, is artistically embodied. No straight reporting, this is a story conceived and executed with a fiction writer's talent.

By the time Agee published "A Mother's Tale," fifteen years later, that talent had come to fruition. This story, a haunting allegory told by a mother cow to her inquisitive calf, is about The One Who Came Back and The Man With The Hammer. The strange probing parables of Franz Kafka come immediately to mind when one reads this story, as does Stephen Crane's *The Red Badge of Courage*. Aside from the mere fact of bovine speech, this story has a Kafkaesque unreality and terror to it. More limited in scope than Crane's work, the tale has essentially the same theme: the reality of war is senseless death, not romantic glory.

This horror story opens with a cow and her calf watching an immense drove of cattle moving eastward to, one presumes, their slaughter. The youngster, finding enchantment in the spectacle, reveals himself as a thinly disguised Henry Fleming, who also moons calf-like at the sight of men marching to destruction. Such glorified vision, however, is for the very young. Mother and The One Who Came Back, like Jim Conklin and Henry Fleming's older companions in Crane's novel, have seen the horrifying skull beneath the skin. It is here that Mother relates her macabre tale. The One Who Came Back, one of the herd, finds himself on a dizzying train ride to, unknown to him, the slaughterhouse. Bovinely waiting for something to happen, he soon discovers that the "wonderful knowledge of being one with all his race meant less and less to him, and in its place came something still more wonderful: he knew what it was to be himself alone, a creature separate and different from any other, who had never been before,

and would never be again."[15] The vision of The One Who
Came Back is a humanistic one, the sudden revelation that
all life—especially one's own—is sacrosanct and more
important than any herd philosophy, ideology, or
societal organization.

The culmination of this vision comes when, prodded
into the slaughterhouse, The One Who Came Back sees
The Man With The Hammer:

> A little bridge ran crosswise above the fences. He stood
> on this bridge with His feet as wide apart as He could
> set them. He wore spattered trousers but from the
> belt up He was naked and as wet as rain. Both arms were
> raised high above His head and in both hands He held
> an enormous Hammer. With a grunt which was hardly
> like the voice of a human being, and with all His strength,
> He brought this Hammer down into the forehead of our
> friend: who, in a blinding blazing, heard from his own
> mouth the beginning of a gasping sigh; then there was
> only darkness.[16]

This Capitalized Killer becomes emblematic of paradoxical
deity; He is both merciless God of Destruction and
personified human evil. He is man's inhumanity to his
fellow man and living creature, man who—like Shiva in
the *Bhagavad Gita*—becomes "death, the Destroyer of
Nations." It is The Man With The Hammer who smites
armies, razes cities, and murders the perishable body.

The One Who Came Back, however, remains a living
testament of Hemingway's truth that "man can be
destroyed, but not defeated." Although the body can be
broken the soul cannot be, and The One Who Came Back
comes back as living proof: "He came up out of the East
as much staggering as galloping (for by now he was so
worn out by pain and exertion and loss of blood that he

could hardly stay upright), and his heels were so piteously torn by the hooks that his hooves doubled under more often than not, and in his broken forehead the mark of the Hammer was like the socket for a third eye."[17] It is because of this "third eye" that The One Who Came Back sees more clearly than before, but again we are confronted by a paradox. One would have hoped that this harrowed traveler had found a deeper understanding of suffering and, thus, greater wisdom and compassion. But this does not prove to be the case. Although there are hints that this forlorn creature is Christ-like (his arrival from the East, his stigmatic hooves, his suffering), his newly acquired knowledge betrays a satanic hatred: *"Never be taken. . . . Never be driven. Let those who can, kill Man. Let those who cannot, avoid him."*[18] He further advises the others to kill the yearlings and the calves: *"So long as Man holds dominion over us . . . bear no young."*[19] Although Man undoubtedly deserves such condemnation, Agee's point seems clear: violence breeds only further violence. The heroism of The One Who Came Back may be commendable, but he remains only a sad, beaten animal. He has failed to learn through suffering, to become truly Christ-like, to become Everyman, or, in his case, Everycow.

Like Hawthorne's "Young Goodman Brown" this story has a dual theme. It is apparent from the tale of the victimized cows that Agee's bovine world, like that of Goodman Brown, is violent, evil, and satanic. But Agee is not writing a sermon against the world, the flesh, and the devil. His major theme is exemplified in The One Who Came Back. Christ-like in his suffering, he—again like Goodman Brown—fails to see life steady and whole. Although man is a bestial creature, he is a noble one too, and to see him as either/or is a gross perversion. The One Who Came Back has learned only cruelty and, as his maxims illustrate, has become cruel himself. One feels that, like Brown, he will have "no hopeful verse upon his tombstone: and that his dying hour will be gloom." The nobility of all creatures, man and cow alike, comes from the feeble attempt to rise above mortality and suffering, from—as Faulkner puts it—their ability to "endure." It is this that Agee tells us through the negative example of The One Who Came Back.

The Morning Watch

The Morning Watch, published in 1951 after first appearing in Marguerite Caetani's *Botteghe Oscure,* is the first long work of fiction that Agee completed. It is, in a small way, an impressive work, disciplined, complex, and endowed with the poetic sweep of Agee's lyrical prose. A transitional work, *The Morning Watch* points backward to the symbolism of "A Mother's Tale" and forward to the poignant childhood recollections of *A Death in the Family*. It offers, as Alan Pryce-Jones has pointed out, "a series of keys to the Agee myth."[20]

Richard, the protagonist of *The Morning Watch,* is Rufus Follet grown six years older. Richard, like Rufus, has experienced a death in the family and can still see "his father's prostrate head, and, through the efforts to hide it, the mortal blue dent in the impatient chin."[21] Both young men are sensitive and intelligent. If *A Death in the Family* is the story of a child's first experience with death and his first step toward manhood, *The Morning Watch* is the story of a young man's initiation into life and the full flowering of that manhood.

The watch that Richard undertakes in this story is the religious service between Maundy Thursday and Good Friday in memory of Christ's words to his sleeping disciples: "What, could ye not watch with me one hour?"

Richard's watch takes place in a Tennessee boys' school in 1923, and the narrative is relatively simple. Richard awakens in early morning, attends the worship service at the Lady Chapel, but finds his spiritual thoughts undermined by pride and the flesh. (Matthew 26:41 is particularly apt: "Watch and pray, that ye enter not into temptation: the spirit indeed is willing, but the flesh is weak.") Becoming "empty of prayer and of feeling," Richard sneaks away to go swimming with two friends, Hobe and Jimmy, indulges in idleness, finds a locust shell, kills a snake, and returns to face his punishment from the school superiors. The main action that takes place in this story is obviously not physical; it is Richard's shifting psyche that is especially important here. Moreover, the merit of this short novel lies not in its "story"—as indeed it does not with any work of literary art—but in Agee's subtle use of symbol, imagery, and diction, and his insight into human experience.

Three symbols stand out in *The Morning Watch:* water, the snake, and the locust shell which Richard picks up during his truancy. These can be understood only in full knowledge of the story's main theme—death and resurrection. In Richard's case, it is his childish notions of piety and his immaturity in general which die, while Richard is reborn as a man and a human being. His problem becomes clear as he prays in darkness early in the story: "O God, he silently prayed, in solemn and festal exaltation: make me to know Thy suffering this day. O make me to know Thy dear Son's suffering this day."[22] It is suffering that Richard learns, the suffering not only of Christ and humanity, but of all living creatures; and from this knowledge comes the wisdom that makes him a truly human creature.

During his morning watch, several things take Richard's mind from thoughts of the crucifixion. The vulgarity of his companions is first and most obvious:

Thrown with fury, a shoe struck the wall next Jimmy's
bed: the noise broke upon Richard with sickening
fright. Then Hobe's voice:

"All right some mothuf - - - - - sonofabitch is agoana
git the livin s - - t beat outn him if I find out who
throwed that!"

"Shet yer God damn mouf," said a coldly intense,
deeper voice at the far end of the dormitory.

"Yeah fer Chrise sakes *shut up,*" said another voice,
as several neutral voices said "Shut up."[23]

Richard's extreme introspection and, consequently,
his realization of human pride in all things spiritual also
defeat his childish attempts to rise above the flesh. He
realizes that his pride in being unlike his companions is
"one of the worst sins of all: the Pharisee."[24] Finally, as
spirit and flesh grapple for control within Richard, flesh
often emerges victorious. Thinking of Christ's wounds,
Richard recalls another wound, "a rawly intimate glimpse
he had had, three or four years before, of Minnielee
Henley when they were climbing a tree."[25] "Hell of a saint
I'd make," Richard finally concludes.[26]

It is the final section of this three-part story that
contains some of Agee's finest writing and his most
complex symbolism. As Richard, Hobe, and Jimmy walk
toward the swimming hole, a rooster crows three times.
One immediately recalls the New Testament rooster whose
call signaled Peter's renunciation of Christ. But what is
being renounced in Agee's story? It is certainly not
Richard's faith, for he becomes more "religious" by the
end of the story. More likely it is his childish past that this
cock is crowing an end to. A clearer symbol is the cleansing
water that Richard leaps into. It is Conrad's "destructive
element," the sea of experience into which all must
inevitably plunge, as well as the waters that cleanse away
all sins of pride and ignorance. In the deadly darkness of

this water, Richard becomes "aware of the entire surface of his body as if it were fire" and he wishes to lie forever "against the deepest trench of the bottom, his belly foundering in ooze, his eyes shut, staying his hands on rocks."[27] It is a kind of death by water that Richard undergoes, and his emergence is another resurrection—his body blazes "with pleasure in its existence." "I could have died, he realized almost casually. *Here I am!* his enchanted body sang. I could be dead right now, he reflected in sleepy awe. *Here I am!*"[28] No longer half in love with easeful martyrdom, Richard has come to realize the beauty of being alive.

A more complex symbol is the snake, "more splendid than Richard had ever seen before," which is symbolic of all that is "royally dangerous and to be adored and to be feared, all that is alien in nature and in beauty."[29] A snake suggests the serpent in Eden but, more than this, the snake is Christ. Smashed to death by Richard in a moment of bravado and pity, the snake undergoes the same agonies as Christ on the same day of His suffering, Good Friday. Like Christ, it cannot die until sundown and its blood becomes emblematic of all suffering: Richard wants the snake's blood on his hands "to clear gradually and naturally, the way the smudge clears from the forehead on Ash Wednesday."[30] And, finally, the snake becomes synonymous with the body and blood of Christ. Insensitive Hobe slings the snake's mangled body to the hogs, which promptly gobble it up. It occurs to Richard that the snake is still alive "and would stay alive in their bellies, however chewed, and mangled, and diffused by acids, until the end of the day."[31] The Christ-like serpent not only died for Richard's sins but also served to initiate Richard into manhood. Through the initiation rite of snake-killing, Richard has gained self-respect and the acceptance of his companions. Moreover, he has had a visible and

memorable experience of suffering that has made him
more human. Richard, in a sense, has become Christ-like
himself, for he now identifies with all suffering creatures.
Stumbling on a root on the way back to school, Richard
says to himself, "Jesus falls for the first time," thus
identifying himself with both Christ and serpent.

The final important symbol is the locust shell,
"transparent silver breathed with gold, the whole back
split, the hard claws, its only remaining strength."[32]
Another death and resurrection, this locust has slipped its
shell to rise again. Symbolic of the resurrection of all
living things, the locust rests against Richard's heart as the
story ends. It will, one assumes, serve to remind Richard
of all attempts to rise from the shell of earthly limitation
and open his heart to all that is beautiful, noble, and
dignified in human experience.

The Morning Watch is the first full fruition of the
creative talent that lay dormant in Agee's reportorial
works. It is an impressive short novel—and, one must
remember, a first one—which reveals a tightly controlled
set of images and symbols. Its major failing is perhaps its
introspective quality; the long middle section, full of
brooding, prayer, and religious fervor, often fails to sustain
the reader's interest. Taken as a whole, however, the work
is an example of the remarkable craftsmanship which Agee
was capable of when he disciplined his emotions. Finally,
The Morning Watch is a good introduction to Agee's
masterpiece, *A Death in the Family,* for in the former
one finds the thematic material for the latter.

A Death in the Family

In many ways, *A Death in the Family* is a strangely
anachronistic novel. In the early 1950's, while writers like
Norman Mailer, J. D. Salinger, Saul Bellow, and

Tennessee Williams were asserting the alienation of modern man and the abnormalities of human nature, Agee was at work on a novel affirming the virtues of middle-class family life, the idyllic world of the American small town, and the faith and love of simple people. Such affirmation was, of course, being made—by writers of Book-of-the-Month Club best-sellers—but the work was invariably sentimental tripe. Agee's triumph lay in the fact that he was able to affirm without becoming maudlin and without falsifying his vision of human experience.

Dwight Macdonald correctly points out that the theme of *A Death in the Family* is "the confrontation of love," which he defines as "life carried to its highest possible reach," and death, which he sees as "the negation of life and yet a necessary part of it."[33] Many readers place too much emphasis on "death" and fail to realize that "family" dominates the book. Not solely about death at all, *A Death in the Family* is essentially about love. Various kinds of love, exemplified by each character's relationship to others, to himself, and to the universe, are explored throughout the novel, and the function of Jay Follet's death is partially to elicit responses which help to define these fundamental human emotions. A partial list of the relationships in the book and the characters who exemplify them may give the reader some idea of this theme:

1. divine love (Mary's piety; Aunt Hannah's faith; Father Jackson's inhuman religiosity).
2. husband-wife (Jay and Mary Follet; Joel and Catherine Lynch).
3. child-parent (Mary, Andrew, and the Lynches; Rufus, Catherine, and the Follets).
4. brother-sister and brother-brother (Rufus and Catherine; Andrew and Mary; Ralph and Jay).
5. friendship (Walter Starr; Aunt Hannah and Mary).

6. self-love (Father Jackson, whose self-centered
   devotion to the church cuts him off from human
   concerns; Andrew, whose lack of faith isolates him
   from humanity).

All these relationships, of course, do not fall into easy
categories. They are extremely complex, as human
relationships invariably are, and often shade into one
another. Agee's analysis of marital love, for example,
particularly Jay and Mary's relationship, also includes
divine love (Mary's piety and Jay's lack of faith have been
barriers to their complete understanding of one another)
and self-love (Jay's loneliness and Mary's solace in
religiosity illustrate their inability to escape themselves).
The Follets' marriage is further qualified by the Lynches'.
Joel and Catherine Lynch are, in general, the Follets
grown older, wiser, and more understanding. There is in
their relationship a lack of overt communication
(Catherine's deafness suggests this), but there is a tacit
communication that irrevocably joins them together.
Sitting with her husband, Catherine feels "a moment of
solemn and angry gratitude to have spent so many years,
in such harmony, with a man so good," while Joel feels "a
moment of incredulous and amused pride in her immense
and unbreakable courage."[34] Taken together, the Follets
and the Lynches form a composite study of marital love,
with its joy, frustration, loneliness, and understanding.
If there is paradox here, it is perhaps because life itself is
paradoxical. Just as there are no simple relationships in
life, so are there none in *A Death in the Family*.

The second major theme of the novel is, like so much
of Agee's writing, religious. The bereavement of the Follet
family is more than the personal sorrow of particular
individuals. Beyond this is a higher level of meaning, the
meaning inherent in the Christian doctrine of Original Sin,

the anguish felt by Job when asked, "Canst thou by searching find out God?" The problem, then, that Agee asks us to consider is "What is man's proper religious attitude when faced with earthly hardship and the fact of certain extinction?" Each of the major characters of the book presents a different attitude toward this basic human question, and again a partial listing might prove helpful to the reader:

1. mysticism (the return of Jay's "spirit" in chapter twelve is an example of the mystical experience).
2. rational faith (Aunt Hannah).
3. emotional faith (Mary).
4. devotion to church (Father Jackson).
5. determinism (Joel Lynch).
6. agnosticism (Andrew).
7. atheism (Jay).

Between Jay's apparent atheism ("He wasn't a *Christian*, you know," Andrew reminds Mary) and the mystical experience of Jay's "return," which together represent a direct confrontation of the spiritual and the material worlds, lies almost the entire range of human speculation about what T. S. Eliot, in "Burnt Norton," called "the still point of the turning world," that sense of the absolute which we all must confront sooner or later. Life is a "tale told by an idiot . . . signifying nothing," Joel Lynch claims, by way of Shakespeare, while Andrew believes that it signifies something, "but we don't know what."[35] Mary takes solace in prayer and piety, while Aunt Hannah finds earthly affliction something that "just has to be lived through."[36] Each has taken a particular stand toward God and the human predicament.

Finally *A Death in the Family* is the story of the maturation of Rufus Follet. The story is his, and it is through his eyes that we see the major part of the action.

It is, moreover, Rufus' attitude toward his parents, in
the time that he lived among them "so successfully
disguised to [him]self as a child," that remains in the
foreground:

> I hear my father; I need never fear.
>   I hear my mother; I shall never be lonely,
> or want for love . . . .
>   I hear my father and my mother and they are my
> saints, my king and my queen, beside whom there are no
> others so wise or worthy or honorable or brave or
> beautiful in this world.
>   I need never fear: nor ever shall I lack for
> loving-kindness.[37]

Rufus envisions his parents as the Big People who care
for him, feed and clothe him, and are always there
when needed. The death of his father destroys this idyllic
existence and, paradoxically, also allows Rufus to take
his first step toward manhood. By the end of the novel,
Rufus is no longer the child who is teased and fooled by the
neighborhood bullies. He has come to understand what
death is and, through this understanding, what life
is. His final vision of a giant butterfly moving its wings
"so quietly and grandly" is a vision of human existence,
both beautiful and terrifying. He has, in short, become
a man.

These three rich and complex themes move throughout
the novel like musical motifs, interacting with one
another, qualifying, exploring. In Agee's very believable
world, everyday people confront the same fundamental
issues as the rest of us, struggle with them as we all do, and
react the same as we do in our own lives. This clear and
immediate glimpse into our own existence, which James
Agee has momentarily captured and held with words,

is his great achievement as an artist and the essence of all great art.

A Death in the Family consists of three parts. Part I, chapters one through seven, we might call "The Follet Family: Knoxville, 1915." Part II, chapters eight to thirteen, is "Jay Follet's Death," and Part III, chapters fourteen to twenty, is "Jay Follet's Resurrection." Interspersed throughout these chapters are long sections, set off by italics, which Agee apparently intended to embody within the text. His early death left this work undone. These added sections, however, contain some of the best writing in the novel. The opening, for example, "Knoxville: Summer 1915," is a magnificent piece of measured prose-poetry which is as evocative of American life as anything written in the twentieth century. Here and in other passages, Agee tells us not only what it is like to be at a particular place (Knoxville) at a particular time (1915), but also what it is like to be a child and an American.

No mere summary of plot can fully convey the complexity and interrelationships of characters and themes in *A Death in the Family*. The novel has an almost symphonic arrangement, and anyone who has listened to Samuel Barber's *Knoxville: Summer of 1915* knows how readily Agee's prose can be set to music. In musical terms, the novel is a set of variations on the themes of love and death, Agee's *Tod und Verklärung*.

What is equally difficult to convey is Agee's cinematic technique in the novel. One must remember that while writing *A Death in the Family* he was also at work on screenplays, and this influence upon his writing is profound. The novel abounds in long sections of dialogue, vivid cinematic descriptions, and techniques usually associated with drama and motion pictures. The structure of *A Death in the Family,* not only symphonic, is also the pyramid

structure of the drama, a rising and falling action. The story
leads up to the death of Jay Follet, the apex of the
plot, and the remainder of the book resolves the conflicts
caused by his death.

Finally, sections of the novel, those italicized parts
which Agee did not incorporate into the text, are
seemingly not essential to the main narrative. One feels,
however, that the book would have been poorer without
them, and the sections do serve further to qualify the major
characters. Two scenes, the one in which the Follets
visit Rufus' great-great-grandmother and the one in which
Rufus is taunted about his name by the older boys on
the block, are among the most memorable in the novel.

The visit to grandma's is Rufus' major confrontation
with old age, and it furthers his development toward
maturity. We see the scene through Rufus' eyes, but Agee
blends in with extraordinary subtlety a more mature
vision and consciousness. The scene essentially uses the
Jamesean "central consciousness," a central narrator
whose focus of attention is slightly shifted to allow the
reader a more sophisticated awareness of the scene's
implications. We see, for example, Ralph Follet from
Rufus' viewpoint, but we judge him in a way that would
never occur to Rufus. Ralph is still the Ralph of other
scenes, gregarious, boisterous, insecure, and jealous. He
stands on the running board of the car to give Jay
directions and predictably loses his way. " 'Reckon my
memory ain't so sharp as I bragged,' " he says.[38]
Despite Ralph, the party reaches the "great, square-logged
gray cabin" in the hills and is immediately greeted by
grandma's companion, Great Aunt Sadie, a woman with
big masculine hands, "hard black eyes," and a "dim
purple splash all over the left side of her face."[39]

It is grandma, however, who is the center of attention.
She is a vividly unpreserved woman of one-hundred-three

who smells like "new mushrooms and old spices and sweat."[40] Urged by the adults, Rufus announces his identity to her and kisses "her paper mouth." It is a symbolic kiss of youth and age, the coming-together of life at two disparate poles, and each participant takes on added love from the other. Grandma, "filled with grave intensity," holds Rufus by the shoulders with hands "like knives and forks of ice," makes gurgling noises in her throat, and looks at him with "giggling, all but hidden eyes." Rufus swells "with sudden love" and kisses her again. Theirs is the embrace of humanity, a love of human existence. In a final Joycean image, the "water" that crawls along the dust from under grandma's chair, Agee depicts the elemental waters of life, a visible sign of human ecstasy, and a hint of the cyclical regeneration of all earthly existence. Just as grandma waters the ground, so do we through death become the stuff from which new life springs.

In contrast to grandma's humanity is the cruelty of the Knoxville neighborhood bullies. They are so deceitful and so mean that Rufus wonders how "he could ever grow up to be one of them," though he feels they are "somehow of the same race."[41] Their cruelty is that of the tyrant who depersonalizes human identity. To these "kind-looking, serious boys," Rufus is a "nigger"— a dehumanized thing—a name they yell "after the backs of colored children and even grown-up colored people." The meanness of the world outside the Follet home drives Rufus more deeply into himself. Although he wants to feel that he is "not alone, but one of them," Rufus seems destined to be a lonely person like his father, one more indication that children are their fathers reborn.

Between these extremities of compassion and cruelty lies Rufus' world. To embrace one without the other would be to live a less than fully conscious life. To ignore

the Knoxville bullies is to live a lonely existence:
the more alone Rufus feels, Agee tells us, the more he
wants to feel that he is one of them. To embrace the
world outside is to become less than human. It is only
when armed with grandma's humanity that Rufus can
face the world with compassion, understanding, and
acceptance. It is only when cognizant of the world's
cruelty that he understands the need for compassion.

It is impossible to read *A Death in the Family* without
feeling the author's immense compassion and concern
for his fictional characters. Some readers, however, believe
that this is precisely what mars the novel. Agee, they
say, was too closely identified with his characters and
was unable to achieve the proper detachment necessary to
all great works of art.[42] Such criticism, I feel, is wrong.
It is because of Agee's involvement, his overwhelming
concern for his fictional creations, that the reader is able
to envision the Follets and Lynches as living human beings
instead of allegorical figures. A labor of love, *A Death
in the Family* moves us because it moved its author.

Since *A Death in the Family* is largely Rufus Follet's
story, it is with him we must begin any analysis of
characterization. Rufus, at the time of his father's death,
is six years old. In "Knoxville: Summer 1915," however,
we hear the voice of a much older Rufus Follet looking
back on those earlier days. The purpose of this
reminiscence, as he tells us at the close of this section,
is to find out who he is. The novel reveals that his
search was, at least partially, successful. Early in the novel,
Rufus' sensibilities are those of any six-year-old child:
he is ignorant of death and human suffering, unaware
that he is being made a fool of by the neighborhood
bullies, and blissfully content in his idyllic family circle.
But he is not, by any means, an average child. He is
more sensitive, compassionate, and intelligent than the

other Knoxville children he encounters, and he is a reflective and inquisitive child. These qualities are illustrated in chapter five when Rufus has a lengthy breakfast-table discussion with his mother about the human condition. Concerned about the possible death (although Rufus does not yet fully comprehend this word) of his "Grampa" Follet, he recalls two recent incidents: the death of his cat Oliver and the violent death of several rabbits by savage dogs. "Why did God let the dogs get in?" Rufus inquires.[43] Why God lets the dogs get in is the basic philosophical problem of the novel, and one that is never truly resolved. The fact that Rufus presents us with this question reveals that he too is struggling with the problems of human existence.

By the end of the novel, Rufus has come to see life more deeply and more clearly. When confronted with the death of his father, he is no longer ready to accept his elders' vague comments about God's will and divine mercy. After hearing that his father died of a brain concussion, Rufus replies, "Then it was that, that put him to sleep"—not God. We alone, Rufus has come to realize, are the world we walk in, and divinity lies in things of this world.

The final four chapters are perhaps the most important in the book. It is here that Rufus slowly, almost step by step, gropes his way toward an understanding of life and death. The beginning of this mature knowledge comes when Rufus views, for the last time, his father's body, finding in him a "perfected beauty," something "dry, light, unreal, and touched with a kind of warmth and impulse and a kind of sweetness which felt like the beating of a heart."[44] For the first time in Rufus' young life, he has come face to face with human death. Moreover, he has come to comprehend "in its specific weight the word, dead."[45] No longer just a word, it is a reality—his father—the word made flesh. The room where his father lies feels "like a boundless hollowness in the house and in his own being, as if he stood in the dark near the edge of an abyss and could feel that droop of space in darkness."[46]

Although Rufus now comprehends death in a personal sense, he has yet to comprehend this phenomenon in the wider context of life itself. This final step comes later, after his father's actual burial (which Rufus is not allowed to see), when Andrew and Rufus go for a walk that evening. Feeling honored because "Andrew had never invited him to take a walk with him before," Rufus listens intently to his uncle's story of the burial:

"There were a lot of clouds," his uncle said, and continued to look straight before him, "but they were blowing fast, so there was a lot of sunshine too. Right when they began to lower your father into the ground, into his grave, a cloud came over and there was a shadow just like iron, and a perfectly magnificent butterfly settled on the—coffin, just rested there, right over the breast, and stayed there, just barely making his wings breathe, like a heart."

Andrew stopped and for the first time looked at Rufus. His eyes were desperate. "He stayed there all the way down, Rufus," he said. "He never stirred, except just to move his wings that way, until it grated against the bottom like a—rowboat. And just when it did the sun came out just dazzling bright and he flew up out of that—hole in the ground, straight up into the sky, so high I couldn't even see him any more." He began to climb the hill again, and Rufus worked hard again to stay abreast of him. "Don't you think that's wonderful, Rufus?" he said, again looking straight and despairingly before him.[47]

LIBRARY ST. MARY'S COLLEGE

Rufus' childish vision of this magnificent butterfly, springing upward and waving its great wings, is a vision of the soul's resurrection, of Christian redemption, and of the defeat of death through human dignity and strength. The symbol of the butterfly on a coffin (the butterfly has long been a standard symbol for the soul) is a perfect vision of life itself, the linking of above and below, spirit and earth, divinity and mankind. This vision, the culmination of Rufus' quest for maturity, causes him to see that life is not meaningless and that death is not defeat—"that lying there in the darkness did not matter so much."[48] Rufus has come to accept the paradoxes of human existence, just as he accepts the paradoxes of Andrew's personality which, as he sees, contains both love and hate. Accepting paradox, life, and death, Rufus, having taken his first step toward manhood, walks all the way home in silence.

Although there is much that we know about Rufus' father, he is—among the major figures—the least clearly depicted character in the novel. We do know that he was thirty-six years old exactly a month and a day before his death. He once worked in a post office in the Panama Canal Zone, where he married Mary Lynch, moved to Knoxville, where he had been raised, tried to teach himself law, had difficulty supporting his family, and was at one time a heavy drinker. But the inner man is more difficult to determine. There is an essential loneliness about him that even young Rufus senses. Walking with his father at the opening of the story, Rufus feels that "although his father loved their home and loved all of them, he was more lonely than the contentment of this family love could help; that it even increased his loneliness, or made it hard for him not to be lonely."[49] He remains, perhaps, a shadowy figure because we see him largely through others' eyes. To

Rufus, he is merely "Father," with all the associations
that the word conveys to a child. To Mary, Jay
is husband and provider. To Ralph, he is the older brother
on whom everyone depends. To Walter Starr, he was
"one of the finest men that ever lived,"[50] but to what
extent we can accept Walter's judgment, made partly to
console the Follet children, is a debatable point. Jay
Follet remains, then, a faintly drawn figure on whom the
novel centers and who elicits the emotions and responses
of the other characters in the novel.

Mary Follet, more clearly depicted than her husband,
is certainly less complex. She is a simple woman and
a good mother. Her one failing is her extreme piety, a
blind faith in the benevolence of God that bars her from
the knowledge of human experience that is gained
through suffering. But just as *A Death in the Family* is
the story of Rufus' maturation, so is it the story of
Mary's. By the end of the novel, she has come "to know
herself, and she gained extraordinary hope in this
beginning of knowledge. She thought that she had grown
up almost overnight."[51] This is at least a hint that
Mary may become truly human and truly religious in
more than a church-going sense of the word. Upon the
arrival of Father Jackson, however, near the end of
the novel, she still symbolically leans very heavily on him
as he helps her downstairs.

However interesting they may be in themselves, the
Lynches serve primarily as a contrast to the Follets. Joel
and Catherine are, in a sense, what the Follets would
have become had Jay lived another thirty years. Their
marital problems are strikingly similar: the Lynches too
have been separated by what Joel calls "the whole stinking
morass of churchiness,"[52] and both seemingly
mismatched couples have been hampered by an outward
lack of communication, symbolically depicted by

Catherine's inability to hear. Joel, like Jay Follet, is also an essentially lonely man, painfully aware "of the steady thirty-years' destruction of all of his own hopes."[53]

We know little about Joel Lynch. Fond of reading Thomas Hardy and *The New Republic,* he is a gruff, cynical man who is in his late sixties or early seventies and is apparently retired. Wavering between agnosticism and atheism, he finds little meaning in the universe other than that which his reason tells him. "I've got to have proof," he says. "And on anything can't be proved, be damned if I'll jump either way."[54] As his sister Hannah tells him, he would not be convinced by "God in a wheelbarrow."[55]

Catherine Lynch is living proof of Ashley Montagu's theory, in "The Natural Superiority of Women," that "it is the function of woman to teach men how to be human."[56] Her silent humanity has partially tempered Joel's rough nature and has made their marriage, as much as possible, a happy one. Catherine is gentle, religious, not overly intelligent, and a bit dull, but her warmth and kindness have more than compensated for any deficiences. Joel instinctively responds to his wife's finer qualities and, by doing so, becomes more human himself.

These two marriages, the Follets' and the Lynches', comprise a study of marital love. Although outward differences of religion, intelligence, and emotional response separate these couples, there is a deeper understanding, beyond explanation, that brings them together in moments of tender amusement, proud gratitude, and unbreakable courage.

Perhaps the most religious and human person in *A Death in the Family,* and at the same time the most doubting and searching, is Aunt Hannah Lynch. She is a composite of all the best traits of the other characters. She has Mary's intense faith, but it is colored by her

brother's sense of searching doubt. She has Catherine's
humanity, but it is a more expressive and active kind.
Catherine can only sit and smile, while Hannah clearly
communicates. Aunt Hannah brings to Rufus the
understanding he needs (as well as a new cap), to Mary
the solace she requires, and to Jay's mourners the
stability that maintains their emotional control. Her faith
goes beyond Mary's blind piety, for it is a faith in
humanity and in life itself. "I want to *know* when I die,"
she thinks, "and not just for religious reasons."[57] It is
this complete awareness of life, of both its pain
and pleasure, that makes Hannah one of the most vividly
human characters in the novel. Although others find
kindness in Catherine Lynch, they seek comfort in time
of need from Aunt Hannah.

Among the secondary characters in the novel, Andrew
Lynch and Ralph Follet are the most fully developed.
Andrew, Mary Follet's twenty-three-year-old brother, is a
young man of artistic ambitions and sensitivity. He
is fond of romantic posturing and thinks of himself as
Shelley, "praying for gratitude for being alive."[58] He also
has something of Shelley's agnosticism and sees life
as signifying "something, but we don't know what." And,
finally, like a stereotyped romantic, he is half in love
with easeful death. A brief encounter with Walter Starr,
shortly after their return from the scene of Jay's
accident, reveals not only this attitude, but a profound
insecurity: "Their eyes met, and for a moment both were
caught in astonishment. *He wishes it was me!* Andrew
thought. He wishes it *was himself!* Walter thought.
Perhaps I do, too, Andrew thought, and once again, as he
had felt when he first saw the dead body, he felt absurd,
ashamed, guilty almost of cheating, even of murder, in
being alive."[59] One feels that if Rufus has somehow
become more of a man by the end of the novel, Andrew

has become less. Andrew's lack of faith—in himself,
in life, or in God—has hardened him, alienated him, and
made him more confused. Rufus clearly sees that Andrew,
while talking about his family, "hated all of them."[60]
One can make a good case that there is as much of James
Agee in Andrew Lynch as there is in Rufus Follet.
Doubt, guilt, and artistic development, the concerns of
Andrew, concerned his creator as well, and there
is the strong suspicion that Andrew's paradoxical nature
is also partially Agee's.

Ralph Follet, probably the most unlikeable person in
the novel (Father Jackson is also a candidate), is
certainly the most pitiable. He is gross, fat, fond of drink,
self-pitying, and jealous of his brother Jay's independence
and manhood. Ralph even drives a Chalmers because
it is "a better class of auto and a more expensive one
than his brother's, a machine people made no smart jokes
about."[61] He has, as he realizes, "no courage, no
intelligence, no energy, no independence."[62] Ralph has
remained at home, near his parents, bolstering himself with
alcohol and running his modest undertaker's parlor
"in the hope that by staying near, by always being on hand
if he was needed, by always showing how much he
loved them, he might at last be sure he had won their
approval, their respect."[63] But there is little respect even
from his wife Sally and their son, Jim-Wilson, "and
it was respect he needed, infinitely more than love."[64]
It is Ralph who needlessly lures Jay to his father's home,
hence to his death. It is Ralph who exemplifies the
weakness of human nature, while others illustrate the
strength. And it is Ralph who, of all the characters, is the
most pitiable. Although Jay Follet literally loses his
life, it is his brother who is truly dead (it is fitting that
his life's work is caring for the dead), who reminds
us that there is considerable life to be lost by living.

Two other characters deserve attention: Father Jackson
and Walter Starr. They are most vividly depicted
toward the end of the novel, in closely related scenes, and
are clearly meant to contrast with one another. Father
Jackson, who has come specially from Chattanooga
to perform Jay's burial service, is "a tall stranger in black,
with a frightening jaw and a queer hat."[65] He is a
frowning, distant man with a voice that "loved its own
sound, inseparably from its love of sound and contour
of the words it spoke, as naturally as a fine singer delights
inseparably in his voice and in the melody he is
singing."[66] Children are naturally quick to spot a phony,
and Rufus and Catherine immediately see that there
is "something evil" about Jackson. Later, during the burial,
Father Jackson refuses to read the complete service
over the body because Jay had never been baptized.

Walter Starr, who arrives at the Follet home shortly
after Father Jackson, is a marked contrast. Walter, who
earlier in the novel took Andrew to the scene of
Jay's accident, consoles the children, kindly assists the
Follets, and reveals his humanity in all that he does. It is
he who displays true Christian virtues—kindness,
charity, and humility—while Father Jackson, under the
guise of religion, slowly destroys his own soul. Godliness is
not necessarily churchliness, and it is Walter Starr who
serves as reminder. As for Father Jackson, he is
best summarized by Andrew Lynch, who claims that the
butterfly on Jay's coffin "has got more of God in him
than Jackson will ever see for the rest of eternity."[67]

Other characters appear in *A Death in the Family,* but
their development is slight. Rufus' sister Catherine,
for example, appears as only a shadowy background
figure. She understands nothing of what is going on, and
her only reaction to most situations is to cry. Other
characters—Grandma and Grandpa Follet, Aunt Sadie,

Victoria—appear largely to elicit responses from the more major characters. The novel, then, revolves mainly about a closely knit family unit, and in this consciously restricted group Agee has managed to project a remarkably large range of human experience and emotion. If the function of the novelist is to reveal the life that we know and to give us new insights into that life, then James Agee has, through a glimpse into the lives of only a few characters, given us a glimpse into universal human experience.

Although *A Death in the Family* is Agee's finest achievement, it is an odd book to have appeared in the 1950's and in America. It touches upon no contemporary social problems or minor psychological ones, and it ignores the modern concern with bedroom, boredom, and brutality. It is, moreover, a conservative book stylistically, with no technical innovations or mythopoetic complexity. The author tells his tale simply and lyrically in a straightforward narrative. And finally the theme of the novel is commonplace in modern literature: it is primarily the story of a young man's maturation, and as such stands with Lawrence's *Sons and Lovers,* Joyce's *Portrait of the Artist as a Young Man,* Wolfe's *Look Homeward, Angel,* and Salinger's *Catcher in the Rye.*

What then, we must ask, makes *A Death in the Family* the excellent novel that it is? Jack Behar finds that the book "has a kind of parabolic significance, and even universal import, but no achieved weight and depth, movement and development."[68] But Behar misses the point. Agee's novel is a successful work of literary art largely because of its craftsmanship, the rich pattern of significance that emerges from the structure and the language of the novel. *A Death in the Family* is a tightly constructed work (despite the italicized portions

Agee never wove into the whole), with the dramatic
structure and tension of a play and the lyrical intensity
of a poem. The plot of the novel is simple, but its
simplicity is the deceptive kind of much great literature—
for example, Jane Austen's *Pride and Prejudice*. Agee's
novel, like Austen's, contains no violent scenes or
melodramatic adventures, but both novels contain an
infinity of intimate and realistic details of domestic life.
Again, both novelists reveal, beneath the surface
of their simple narrations, a profound knowledge of the
complex relationships and motivations of people. But by
consciously selecting a relatively simple plot, neither
Agee nor Austen sacrificed novelistic technique. *A Death
in the Family* relies upon balance and antithesis for
its structural pattern, and the pattern of the book is
infinitely complex. For example, the novel opens with
Rufus and his father walking the Knoxville streets
and closes with Rufus and Andrew doing the same. The
early reactions of the Follets to the possible death
of Jay's father foreshadow the reactions of the family to
Jay's actual death. Jay's loneliness and desire to return to
the idyllic world of childhood (although he realizes that
"you never really get all the way home again in your
life"[69]) is a direct contrast to Rufus' loneliness and desire
to escape the world of childhood. Numerous characters
balance one another: the Follets and the Lynches, Rufus
and Andrew, Walter Starr and Father Jackson, Ralph and
Jay. It is this complex pattern, coupled with a functional
prose that conveys the exact pace, rhythm, and
tone of the story, that makes *A Death in the Family* an
outstanding artistic achievement.

Secondly, the book's value lies in what Henry James
called the amount of "felt life" in the novel—in this
case, American life. *A Death in the Family* is a specifically
American novel, so much a part of our unique

tradition and language that it would seem impossible for
a European to share its private vision. Eleanor Steber,
one of America's foremost opera singers, remembers
playing Samuel Barber's *Knoxville: Summer of 1915* for a
cultured German lady who could not understand why
Agee used expressions like "we all lie there, my aunt, my
uncle, my father, my mother." "To her," says Miss
Steber, "it could all have been simplified into a
matter-of-fact sentence or two."[70] It is this quality, this
sense of childhood, family protection, and small-town
revery, that is uniquely American. No one raised in an
American town can read the opening section of the
novel without recognizing part of himself and his own
childhood:

> We are talking now of summer evenings in Knoxville,
> Tennessee in the time that I lived there so successfully
> disguised to myself as a child. It was a little bit mixed sort
> of block, fairly solidly lower middle class, with one
> or two juts apiece on either side of that. The houses
> corresponded: middle-sized gracefully fretted wood houses
> built in the late nineties and early nineteen hundreds,
> with small front and side and more spacious back yards,
> and trees in the yards, and porches. . . .
>   It is not of the games children play in the evening that
> I want to speak now, it is of a contemporaneous
> atmosphere that has little to do with them: that of the
> fathers of families, each in his space of lawn, his shirt
> fishlike pale in the unnatural light and his face nearly
> anonymous, hosing their lawns. The hoses were attached at
> spiggots that stood out of the brick foundations of the
> houses. The nozzles were variously set but usually so there
> was a long sweet stream of spray, the nozzle wet in
> the hand, the water trickling the right forearm and the
> peeled-back cuff, and the water whishing out a long

> loose and low-curved cone, and so gentle a sound. First an
> insane noise of violence in the nozzle, then the still
> irregular sound of adjustment, then the smoothing into
> steadiness and a pitch as accurately tuned to the size
> and style of stream as any violin.[71]

The simple detail of fathers hosing their lawns is enough
to evoke in an American a complex of emotions and
reminiscences. Nor can an American read the brilliant
descriptions of motion pictures, William S. Hart "with both
guns blazing and his long, horse face and his long, hard
lip" and Charlie Chaplin, "squattily walking with his toes
out and his knees wide apart, as if he were chafed," or the
descriptions of the L & N Railroad Depot, or the market
bar with its smell of "beer, whiskey and country bodies,
salt and leather," without recognizing something
specifically American, a mood, a tempo, and an
atmosphere unlike that of any other nation.

The novel is valuable, too, for the insights into human
nature that it gives us. Fiction, involving more than plot,
character, and structure, does not exist in a vacuum.
It touches in clearly discernible ways the life of man,
holding the mirror up to his human personality and, at
times, radically changing it. *A Death in the Family* achieves
a high level of human insight because it focuses on portions
of human experience that we all recognize: death,
childhood, and parental love. One of the major themes of
the novel is death and resurrection. Jay's soul is spiritually
reborn in the form of a butterfly at the end of the novel,
but it is also physically reborn in Rufus. There is a sense
in which all fathers are born again in their sons, and it is
this transformation that Rufus has undergone. Jay reveals
throughout the novel an innate loneliness and a strong
desire to return to the idyllic (though perhaps idyllic only
in retrospect) life of childhood. Jay's desire is achieved

when Rufus, whose loneliness links him spiritually as well as physically to his father, attains partial manhood. If Rufus has become more like his father by the end of the novel, Jay Follet has been born again in his son. This, then, is the allegory of *A Death in the Family*. Jay Follet's death and rebirth in his son Rufus is the eternal pattern of human experience, the never-ending regeneration of the human spirit. Each of us is a portion of his father and, as such, a portion of all men. What Rufus truly seeks is identity ("who are you, child, who are you, do you know who you are, do you know who you are, child; are you?"[72]) with which he can face the world. We recognize in Rufus Follet a part of ourselves because he represents childhood in general. Perhaps only *Huckleberry Finn* conveys so vividly the essential loneliness of childhood, the fact that the child whom we all inhabit is "only the cruelest of deceits."[73] Like Huck Finn, Rufus uses the word "lonely" time and again, and at the core of his experience is a profound loneliness, present from the very beginning of the novel and heightened by the death of his father. The mere fact that Rufus is a child, with a child's vision, thoughts, and perspective, sufficiently alienates him from his family, and his extreme sensitivity and immaturity create an unbridgeable gap between him and the neighborhood children. "The more alone he felt," we are told, "the more he wanted to feel that he was not alone, but one of them."[74] Through the death of his father, who—like Christ—dies so that others might live, Rufus finds identity and attains an adult vision of human experience. Although we cannot say that Rufus Follet has attained adulthood, we can claim that he has undergone the necessary maturing experience and is now prepared to take on adulthood.

And finally there is the human emotion at the core of the novel which conveys not only the feelings of particular people at a particular time, but the universal

feelings of all people at all times. We see, in a few intimate
glimpses of the Follets, one of the outstanding examples
in modern fiction of the intimacy of married life, not
merely in its moments of sexuality (there is, in fact,
surprisingly little sexuality in the book) but in the
commonplace moments which bring a man and woman
closely together. When Jay prepares to leave home in the
middle of the night to visit his father, we see just such an
intimate moment when he smooths the sheets of the bed
for Mary while she is cooking his breakfast and draws
the covers up "to keep the warmth" until she can return to
bed. The scene is slightly ironic, for the warmth will leave
Mary's life forever once Jay departs. But it is this scene
and others which force us once again to conclude that
not all relationships in the twentieth century are sordid,
that deep and binding love between husband and wife is
still possible. The Follets' moments of silent
communication, when both feel "almost the shyness of
courtship," and the moments when Mary looks at Jay "as
if he were her son" and Jay responds toward "her
innocence of this motherliness"[75] are precisely the times
when we, as readers, recognize in them a sizable portion of
ourselves. James Agee said the following in *Let Us Now
Praise Famous Men:*

> [Each of us] is intimately connected with the bottom and
> the extremest reach of time:
>   Each is composed of substances identical with the
> substance of all that surrounds him, both the common
> objects of his disregard, and the hot centers of stars:
>   All that each person is, and experiences, and shall never
> experience, in body and in mind, all these things are
> differing expressions of himself and of one root, and are
> identical: and not one of these things nor one of these
> persons is ever quite to be duplicated, nor replaced, nor has

it ever quite had precedent: but each is a new and
incommunicably tender life, wounded in every breath, and
almost as hardly killed as easily wounded: sustaining,
for a while, without defense, the enormous assaults of the
universe.[76]

In the unique life of each of us lies the common root of
humanity. In *A Death in the Family,* Agee has shown,
through the transparency of fiction, how each of us is
linked one to another through the common bond of
that humanity.

agee on film

V

*One foresees the sad day, indeed,
when Agee on Films will be the
subject of a Ph.D. thesis.*
—*W. H. Auden*, Agee on Film

When James Agee turned to motion
pictures in the late forties and early fifties, there was a
certain predictability in the gesture. His work up to that
point had always had a cinematic basis—a style, pace, and
vision not unlike that found in the motion picture. We
know from his earliest letters that Agee harbored ambitions
to work in films, particularly as a director, and we can see
that he was constantly concerned with mediums that would
reproduce, with pictorial exactness, the material
appearance of things. "Words could, I believe, be made to
do or to tell anything within human conceit," he said.
"That is more than can be said of the instruments of any
other art. But it must be added of words that they are
the most inevitably inaccurate of all mediums of record and
communication."[1] But, he continued, when the camera is
"handled cleanly and literally in its own terms, as an
ice-cold, some ways limited, some ways more capable, eye,
it is, like the phonograph record and like scientific
instruments and unlike any other leverage of art, incapable
of recording anything but absolute, dry truth."[2]

It is impossible, however, to say that Agee made a *deliberate* switch to motion pictures. Although he had been leaning for years toward a medium that would capture the outward appearance of his imaginative vision, there is no evidence that the cinema was the climax of an artistic search for expressive form. It is probable that he drifted into the motion picture just as he had previously drifted into journalism and television; it was merely one more commercial venture into which he decided to throw his artistic talents. If there are more intellectual reasons for his venture into Hollywood, however, they are as much sociological and philosophical as they are aesthetic.

What might have been sociological attractions to the film for Agee are best explained by Rudolf Arnheim:

> As the pictorial art of film became a performing art, ..
> it became a part of the stream of daily life, fulfilling
> the needs of the moment, dramatising and reflecting the
> events of the day. It was, as it were, close to the traffic
> of the street, much closer, much more akin to the traffic of
> the street than pictorial art had ever been. And therefore
> in a society which was democratic and capitalistic at the
> same time the medium of the film adapts itself
> democratically to the taste and interests of the masses, and
> it becomes capitalistically an exploitation of the new
> medium as a profitable commercial enterprise. Hence, the
> ambiguity of the status of the film which has existed
> from the beginning in that on the one hand, it was a child
> of the democratic age—it was art created for all men
> for the first time, as it were—and on the other hand, it was
> a cheap mass product of entertainment and perhaps the
> beginning of the end of that aristocratic history which is
> the history of the art of the Western civilization.[3]

In Arnheim's statement one can see many of the same ideas that concerned Agee. Agee's moral consciousness,

his social awareness, his Leftist idealism, and his somewhat
naïve (and essentially American) faith in the masses
combined to make the motion picture, "a child of the
democratic age," a beguiling outlet for his creative talents.
If Trilling is correct in assuming that Agee conceived art to
be "as hopeless a means of expression as journalism,"[4]
then the motion picture was an ideal medium for Agee's
talents. It was directed to the masses, not to the
intelligentsia; it was a pictorial medium, not primarily a
cerebral one; it was a medium capable of conveying the
timeless anguish of the Rickettses and Gudgers when
the tyranny of words failed.

Added to this was another fact that Arnheim again
points out:

> [The film is] mechanically produced, photographically as
> an image of reality. Now this characteristic is more than
> just a technical achievement and particularity; it is
> the expression of a fundamental change of attitude towards
> what is relevant in the visible world. The photographic
> medium embodies an eager aceptance of a mechanical
> realism which is implied in the nature of the photographic
> image. It implies that a new significance is accorded
> to the material surface of events on earth. Now this
> attitude is limited to a few civilizations in the history of
> the world; it is an attitude which we find reflected in
> realistic art. And realistic art is rare in the history of the
> world.[5]

Concerned with representing external objects in their own
terms ("I 'conceive of' my work," he once said, "as an
effort to be faithful to my perceptions."[6]), Agee found the
language of physical reality "the most beautiful and
powerful but certainly . . . about the heaviest of all
languages."[7] For the camera, he continued, "much of this
is solved from the start."[8] What becomes increasingly

evident throughout Agee's scattered critical statements is his distrust of, as well as his love for, words and his awareness of their inability to "impart the deftness, keenness, immediacy, speed and subtlety of the 'reality' "[9] they try to produce.

But Agee was not a mechanical realist. The world was to Agee, as it was to the Symbolists, a vast system of correspondences. Unlike the Symbolists, however, who believed that all material things corresponded to ideas in the world of the spirit, Agee saw material objects as an extension of divinity, the biblical Word made Flesh. Everything, he said in *Let Us Now Praise Famous Men,* is "most significant in proportion as it approaches in our perception, simultaneously, its own singular terms and its ramified kinship and probable hidden identification with everything else."[10] And each human being is "composed of substances identical with the substance of all that surrounds him, both the common objects of his disregard, and the hot centers of stars."[11] All earthly events were intimate transactions between "this home and eternal space,"[12] and they held special importance for Agee. Richard's snake, for example, in *The Morning Watch* or the butterfly in *A Death in the Family* were literally holy, and Agee believed that such divinity could be reflected only by a realistic art, but one that was raised to a higher level than that of the Naturalists:

> I doubt that the straight "naturalist" very well understands what music and poetry are about. That would be all right if he understood his materials so intensely that music and poetry seemed less than his intention; but I doubt he does that, too. That is why his work even at best is never much more than documentary. Not that documentation has not great dignity and value; it has; and as good "poetry" can be extracted from it as from living itself; but the

documentation is not of itself either poetry or music and it is not, of itself, of any value equivalent to theirs. So that, if you share the naturalist's regard for the "real," but have this regard for it on a plane which in your mind brings it level in value at least to music and poetry, which in turn you value as highly as anything on earth, it is important that your representation of "reality" does not sag into, or become one with, naturalism; and in so far as it does, you have sinned, that is, you have fallen short even of the relative truth you have perceived and intended.[13]

The problem for any artist, as Agee saw it, was to express the reality of sensate experience in a medium that could transcend the natural world, that could approach the realm of music and poetry. And it was the motion picture camera that was most capable of this task; the camera was, to Agee, "the central instrument of our time,"[14] a device by which man could rediscover the shape and pattern of his everyday visual experiences. Just as the invention of musical instruments imposed order upon our auditory sense, so does the camera order our visual sense. In an age fractionalized by reason and scientific knowledge, the camera was for Agee the instrument by which man could once again see his world as an organic visual shape. In short, as Marshall McLuhan has stated, the motion picture is a reel creation, which "merges the mechanical and organic in a world of undulating forms."[15]

One feels compelled to justify Agee's career in motion pictures when perhaps no justification is necessary. The motion picture, a child of technology in an age of discord, may yet turn out to be the outstanding dramatic medium of the twentieth century. One has only to think back to the Elizabethan stage, with its ephemeral productions, its vitality, its pandering to the masses, and its supreme genius, to find a similar period of dramatic production.

While drama critics lament the decline of the legitimate theater and literary scholars deplore the vacuity of our present drama, dozens of first-rate films pass before our eyes every year; these films, more effectively than theatrical drama, mirror and unify the disparate visions of our incomprehensible world. It is not improbable that, two hundred years from now, scholars will look back to our age—with the same seriousness and pedantry we now reserve for the Elizabethans—as a great age of drama in films, while we, without benefit of hindsight, deplore the prostitution of the creative people who endeavor to produce it. In fact, an early start in this direction is being made by highly serious film journals such as *Cahiers du Cinéma, Film Comment, Sight and Sound, Film Culture,* as well as a growing list of scholarly books on the art of the film. And it is not just the French, Polish, and Russian "art" films that receive close study, but masterpieces from Alfred Hitchcock, John Huston, and other American directors as well.

James Agee once wrote the following:

If you compare the moving pictures released during a given period with the books published during the same period—or with the plays produced or the pictures painted or the music composed—you may or may not be surprised to find that they stand up rather well. I can think of very few contemporary books that are worth the jackets they are wrapped in; I can think of very few movies, contemporary or otherwise, which fail to show that somebody who has worked on them, in front of the camera or in any one of many places behind it, has real life or energy or intensity or intelligence or talent.

But you have only to compare the best of last year's films with the best that have been made or in your conception could be made, and the best that have been

made with the best work you have known in any other art
you choose, to know that those who make or care for
moving pictures have great reason to be angry, for all that
is frustrated, and still greater reason to be humble, for
all that is fallen short of, frustration or no. And if you
foresee how few years remain before the grandest prospect
for a major popular art since Shakespeare's time
dissolves into the ghastly gelatinous nirvana of television,
I think you will find the work of this last or any recent
year, and the chance of any sufficiently radical
improvement within the tragically short future, enough
to shrivel the heart. If moving pictures are ever going to
realize their potentialities, they are going to
have to do it very soon indeed. Aware of that, and aware
also of the works of genius which have already been
achieved in films, I have no patience with the patient and
patronizing who remind us mellowly that it took
centuries to evolve an Aeschylus or a Joyce.[16]

To those who share Dwight Macdonald's fear of Masscult
and Midcult[17] or deplore, with Clement Greenberg,
America's abundance of *Kitsch*,[18] Agee's statements must
sound horribly naïve. Are not the movies, for the most
part, still gross, slick, and superficial? Is not what
Macdonald calls "the tepid ooze of Midcult"[19] spreading
everywhere? Do we not in America still esteem the
Sandra Dees and Fabians, the John Waynes and the Jimmy
Stewarts? The answer is probably "yes," but it is not as
resounding as it once was. As Agee suggests, one has only
to compare the yearly output of Hollywood productions
with the "legitimate" theatrical productions in New York
to realize that there is little difference between them—in
fact, one must honestly admit, I think, that Hollywood
comes off better. The vapid series of slick, imitative
Broadway musicals and the painfully pretentious and

overblown "serious" dramas show little more creative talent than the best of Hollywood. And we must remember, too, that Broadway—like Hollywood—has its Lunts, Carol Channings, and Barbra Streisands, all of whom are more "personalities" than performers.

The creative period of avant-garde writing in America, largely the first twenty years of our century, seems over (the so-called avant-garde productions of the off-Broadway theater merely rehash techniques that were introduced, many of them in films, years ago). The fact, however, that our creative work is Midcult is not necessarily bad; what is important is the quality of our Midcult and Masscult productions. The novel and the English theater, particularly the Elizabethan theater, were both Midcult genres; both, however, produced masterpieces. The danger to our culture, as Agee clearly foresaw, lay between the extremes of the "gelatinous nirvana of television" (how prophetic his statement seems today!) and the frustrated potentialities of the motion picture. If a truly popular art was to come into being, he clearly saw in 1945, the motion picture would have to realize its potential. Today, I believe that we could say that it has. The once-prevalent grade-B potboilers of the film have been syphoned off into television; the influence of the European film has raised the audience's level of sophistication and has broken down many of those "frustrations" that Agee once lamented. We indeed have, as Macdonald fears, a Midcult art, but whether it is *Kitsch* or not is the essence of the problem; it is a problem that can be resolved only by time and by future historians of American culture.

It is not my purpose in this chapter to become involved in a sociological study of American culture, nor is it my intention to analyze fully Agee's contribution to the motion picture. The former is a task for the historian and the sociologist; the latter, despite W. H. Auden's fear,[20] is a

job for future scholars and writers of doctoral dissertations.
A satisfactory study of Agee's contribution to the film
would require a book in itself. My purpose in this chapter
is literary, not sociological or filmic. I wish to analyze
briefly the scripts and film criticism of James Agee, noting
their general themes, their thought, and their relationship
to Agee's other writings.

Agee's Scripts

Aside from two documentaries, one about Harlem life
and the other about Williamsburg, a Filipino film entitled
Genghis Khan, and a television play based on the life of
Lincoln, Agee wrote five Hollywood scripts upon which his
reputation as a scenarist rests. All but one of them,
Noa Noa, are what Agee called "fiction" films (*Noa Noa* is
perhaps fiction, too, if one stretches the term a bit).
"Nearly all of the most talented people in moving pictures
work in fiction," Agee said, "and most of the greatest
possibilities lie within fiction."[21] Here we are immediately
at the center of Agee's contribution to the film script.
Just as he had a screen writer's approach to fiction, so did
he have a fiction writer's approach to the motion picture.
The following, for example, is a camera direction for a
scene from *Noa Noa,* one in which Gauguin, gone native,
plunges to the bottom of the ocean to hunt, Tahitian
style, for pearls:

> We follow him down to a sea-floor so deep it is semidark
> in crystal water, and among the strange and marvelously
> colored sea-plants and corals he searches out shell-fish,
> for their pearls. He opens the first two with a knife and puts
> the pearls in his mouth. Thenceforth he is too short of
> breath to open the shells; he just cuts them loose and tucks
> them into his *pareu*—which he wears almost as a G-string.
> Suffering for air, he sights still more shells. We intensify to

> maximum the conflict between lack of air, exertion, and
> greed for more pearls. Carrying all the shells he can in
> each hand, plus his knife, and half-asphyxiated, he stands
> upright, settles his feet against knife-edged coral, and
> with all his strength springs upward, his cut feet trailing
> blood.[22]

This is the writing of a man who fears that the visual
image of the screen cannot capture the beauty inherent in
words. It is not functional description (cut to, pan and
track shot, etc.); it is description by a writer in love with
the rhythm and force of words. Agee, I think, ultimately
failed as a script writer because the visual image he sought
was always subordinated to the verbal image he achieved.
His scripts *read* better than they film. He was, in fact,
at his best when he was working with clearly outlined
fictional material. *The Bride Comes to Yellow Sky*
(1951–52), and *The Blue Hotel* (1948–49), both Stephen
Crane stories, are two of his earliest and finest scripts
There is a precision, a tightness, and a unified effect to
each of these that Agee failed to achieve in other, more
original scenarios.

The Bride Comes to Yellow Sky is, as film critic
William S. Pechter has claimed, "perhaps Agee's finest
piece of writing for the screen, and a work of genuine
charm."[23] Faithful to the mood, tone, and theme of Crane's
delightful story, it nonetheless has typical Agee touches.
Scratchy's jibes at respectability and religiosity recall
similar criticisms of such unlikeable figures as Father
Jackson in *A Death in the Family* and the Bishop in *Noa
Noa,* both respectable and villainous bourgeois. Scratchy,
sotted and itching for a fight, declares to the Yellow Sky
townsmen that

> there ain't hardly a man of ye dast *touch* a gun, let alone
> come up again a *man* with one. Oh no! Got lil' ole

honeybunch to worry about, lil' old wifey-pifey, all the
young 'uns, make ye some easy money runnin' a store,
doctorin', psalm-singing, fix ye a purty lawn so Scratchy
kin cut it for ye, if ye can't get a Mex cheap enough. Oh,
I—(he searches helplessly, then half-says)—hate—I
could wipe every one of ye offen the face o' the earth,
a-hidin' behind yore women's skirts, ever' respectable last
one of ye! Come out an' fight! Come on! Come on! Dad
blast ye![24]

The script moves rapidly and has a sense of inevitability
as it shifts from Potter's arrival by train to Scratchy's
drunken shenanigans. Agee plots the collision course of
Potter and Scratchy with ironic accuracy and avoids the
temptation of a Hollywood melodramatic ending. As
in Crane's story, Scratchy shuffles into the sunset, the last
of the old breed, after being confronted with Potter's
bride.

The Blue Hotel is another successful Agee screenplay.
This script was written while Agee was under contract to
Huntington Hartford, but it never reached the screen.
It was, however, adapted for a television production on
Omnibus. Again faithful to Crane's story, it is a moody
piece, swiftly paced and deftly plotted (again Agee was at
his best when he was working with someone else's story).
Agee and Crane diverge briefly in the scene involving
the Swede's death. Tersely accomplished by Crane, the
scene is vivified by Agee through some nervous and intense
shots that cut from one object to another:

LONG SHOT—THE TABLE
Faces and eyes just at the end of casually looking at him;
resuming their private conversation. This shot is as
quick as a glance.

MEDIUM CLOSE SHOT—BARKEEPER
At his station near mid-bar. Eyes quick from the table to

the Swede, a quick size-up; underplayed and, again, as quick as a glance.

CLOSE SHOT—DOWN ON THE SWEDE'S VALISE AND RIGHT FOOT
He plants his right shoe on the rail; it is clogged with snow; he stomps and scrapes rather loudly, trying to clear it.

MEDIUM LONG SHOT—THE TABLE
Quick, gentlemanly glances of annoyed wondering what it is, finding out, gentlemanly ignoring of the boorishness; back to their muttons.

CLOSE SHOT—BARKEEPER
A sharp little glance toward the table and toward the noise; annoyance; a tinge of refinement.

CLOSE DOWN SHOT—VALISE AND FOOT
The Swede gets his foot hung comfortably.[25]

If there is a weakness to the script, it is the same weakness that exists in Crane's story: unnecessary moralizing. Crane's point is clear, and Agee makes it even more so: "Every sin is a collaboration. Everybody is responsible for everything."[26]

The African Queen (1950) was Agee's first full-length and successfully produced fiction film, but to what extent it is solely Agee's is difficult to determine. John Collier, Peter Viertel, and John Huston also share screen credit for the script. It is an entertaining film, certainly Agee's most slickly commercial, but its success is probably due as much to Huston's direction as it is to the script. As Macdonald points out, the movie contains touches which seem to be Agee's: "the Anglican service with only shining black faces in the congregation, Bogart's stomach rumblings at the tea party, the peculiar horror of the leeches and the gnats."[27] But one can only speculate on

Agee's contribution to this film; to attribute whatever
merit the movie has to Agee alone would be a mistake.
One therefore has to eliminate *The African Queen* from
any final assessment of Agee's contribution to the motion
picture on the grounds that this particular movie is one
of those numerous Hollywood productions which are the
result of talented collaboration.

   The Night of the Hunter (1954) is, I think, the most
successful of Agee's longer, produced screenplays. Based
on a novel by Davis Grubb and directed by Charles
Laughton, the movie has the terror of first-rate Gothic
drama and the magical mood of a kind of grotesque fairy
tale. The Agee touches are evident: Willa, buried
underwater in the car, "her hair wavin' lazy and soft like
meadow grass under flood waters and that slit in her throat
just like she had an extry mouth";[28] the psychopathic
preacher with his hands labeled L-O-V-E and H-A-T-E;
the respectable bourgeois ignorance of Walt and Icey
Spoon. As a film, *The Night of the Hunter* failed to achieve
the potential of the script, but this was not Agee's doing.
William Pechter sees the movie as a directorial failure:

> As a film, *The Night of the Hunter* was a work of such
> magnificent ambition and intransigence as almost to attain
> success by virtue of such magnificence alone. But ambition
> and intransigence are not enough. *The Night of the Hunter*
> is the kind of work which depends for its very existence
> on the sustaining of a mood and a style, the style of
> magic realism; it is as fragile as a fairy tale. Instead, as
> directed by Laughton, the film is of such a clattering
> eclecticism as occasionally to resemble a compressed
> stylistic history of the medium, from flat-lit naturalism to
> Germanic expressionism, from Griffith lyric to Welles
> Gothic. Like Welles, one can imagine Laughton having
> spent a year just seeing movies in preparation for being a

director; unlike Welles, instead of then making his own
film, he seems rather to have decided to remake everybody
else's. Probably the kind of controlled stylistic unity that
such a dreamlike work demands is achieved with less
difficulty in literature, in which all events may be estranged
from us by a veil of language. To achieve this style of
sustained unreality in film one has constantly to resist the
camera's natural propensity for the real, the concrete
object. I have not read the novel of *The Night of the
Hunter;* the film, despite such beautifully realised passages
as the flight down the river, is most often groping
awkwardly for that fitting style it only intermittently
achieves. And Agee's screenplay seems to be caught in some
limbo between the two of them.[29]

Despite Pechter's disappointment, the film does manage
to sustain a delicate balance between adult nightmare and
childhood vision, and, in spite of its eclecticism, it is
perhaps one of the two or three finest "horror" movies
produced in the last two decades.

Agee's final scenario and one which has never reached
the screen is a hotly debated work entitled *Noa Noa,*
based on the South Sea diary of artist Paul Gauguin.
Gauguin's son, Emile, read the script and was reportedly
"delighted by it." He felt "that a true understanding of his
father's spirit and courage had been achieved."[30] Pechter,
however, finds it Agee's "weakest work," a hodge-podge of
clichés of "the noble savage" and the "all-suffering
Christ."[31] The script's true value, I feel, lies somewhere in
between. *Noa Noa* is certainly Agee's most ambitious
script. There are some interesting and artistic shots: "The
Camera is so moved and cut as to make the sign of the
Cross over Gauguin";[32] some unproducible directions:
"Gauguin paints as a hypnotist, imposing his will on it";[33]
and some pontifical asides: "The funeral sequence is to be

cut rigidly to the music of Chopin's Funeral March. I
will indicate the cuts and shots exactly, but serve warning
that without the melody to key it to, it will be hard to
read, or to imagine the effectiveness of."[34] Finally, there is
some unbelievably bad dialogue: "Perhaps the trouble is
that I'm incapable of—sufficient love—for anything.
Except my work."[35] But the script's main weakness lies in
a melodramatic and contrived ending—Gauguin, a kind
of artistic Lord Jim, struggles to free Tahitian natives from
despotic rule—and in some heavy-handed symbolism: "WE
PAN in, close over Gauguin's own, new, nameless, wooden
cross, to the foot of a great Crucifix and the snow-white,
weather-split feet of a wooden Corpus."[36] Rather than a
probing study of a tormented and talented artist, the movie
becomes "The Adventures of Paul Gauguin" or "A
Portrait of the Artist as an Aging Christ." But one cannot
discount the script entirely. There is a sincerity to many
of its passages which seem to have come out of the anguish
of Agee's own life:

GAUGUIN   I shall be dying, I believe, very soon.

VERNIER   (quietly) What is it, Gauguin?

GAUGUIN   My heart.

VERNIER   Is there anything I can do?
Gauguin smiles thanks and shakes his head.

GAUGUIN   (calmly) Nothing.
Vernier glances at Gauguin's feet, as Gauguin starts
lighting up his tobacco.

VERNIER   Are you suffering much pain?
Gauguin forgets the unlighted match . . .[37]

Agee, we recall, had had several of his many heart attacks
by the time he started work on *Noa Noa,* and we know

that he, like Gauguin in his film script, had a "constant
awareness of death, and the shortness of time, and of time
wasted."[38] To Agee, *Noa Noa* was a summing up of his
own artistic career and of his concept of the artistic impulse
that derives from personal suffering. "And yet in all this
lifetime's accounting of losses," he proclaimed through
Gauguin, "I feel a kind of peaceful joy I had never
dreamed could exist for me. I've always tried to be true
to my vocation, come what might. But I begin to realize
that—if I could properly use your language—the real
effort has always been, simply, to be true to my own soul.
And that I have been and now I know the price."[39] Agee,
like Gauguin, was a sufferer, a man who worked tirelessly
while aware of his own potential sudden death, and an
artist who tried only "to be true to [his] own soul." *Noa
Noa* then is of utmost importance to anyone interested in
Agee's development, for in it he put a sizable portion of
himself and the summation of a lifetime.

It is one of the ironies of Agee's career that the medium
toward which he leaned all of his life, the motion picture,
was the one in which he was least successful. His scripts,
taken as a whole, are uneven, often "arty" in the worst
sense of the word, and—in the case of his most ambitious
project, *Noa Noa*—cliché, sentimental, and melodramatic
They are effective, if at all, in print more so than on the
screen. Pechter evaluates the scripts this way:

> The publisher's blurb for the scenarios [in *Agee on Film*]
> has a tendency to argue that they are actually more
> perfectly realized than could be any possible film of them,
> and, in a sense, this is not entirely untrue. The scenarios
> are as fully detailed as any such work could be; every
> nuance has been already indicated by the writer, and any
> director wholly respecting all the scripts' intentions would
> merely be going through Agee's pre-ordained paces,

performing solely as his *alter ego*. The scenarios, as they
were written, were also directed . . . directed, and yet
not filmed. For the actual terrible truth is that, complete
as they are, these scenarios do not exist at all; they have no
more independent existence than an unperformed score
of music. A scenario's only proper life is that of film: just
as film editing corresponds to the writer's final act of
revision, the analogue to the original act of literary
creation is filming. Certain sequences in Agee's screenplays
seem, on the basis of their description, quite remarkable,
and yet one can only say what they *seem* to be, never
what they *are*. For much as Eisenstein "proved" on paper
unprecedented beauties which he was never able to achieve
on film, so what is best in Agee's writing for the screen
remains less part of the history of art than that of
suggestion, speculation, aspiration, passionate desire, and
the ephemera of dreams.[40]

Surely Pechter is wrong in stating that a film script has no
independent existence. Just as a symphony conductor can
hear a score in his mind, so can a reader envision a film
script. It would be more correct to say that a screen
production is an inferior version of that ideal performance
that exists in the imagination. Yet Pechter is on the right
track. Agee's scripts do fail to come alive, perhaps more the
fault of Hollywood than of Agee, and are not lasting
contributions to the film. They self-consciously strive for
effects which they seldom achieve; they aspire to more
than they attain. Agee's films, it is sad to say, will be
remembered, if they are remembered at all, as the works
of a man who tried to push the American motion picture
closer toward a fully developed art form. They remain
on the border of greatness, never quite crossing that
division between the smoothly glittering Hollywood image
of itself and the more profound and honest vision of art.

Agee's Criticism

"It is my business to conduct one end of a conversation, as an amateur critic among amateur critics," James Agee said in one of his first motion picture reviews. "And I will be of use and of interest only in so far as my amateur judgment is sound, stimulating, or illuminating."[41] Seeing himself from this perspective, James Agee claimed no consistent film aesthetic in the volume of random criticisms that now compose *Agee on Film*. He was nonetheless, as Penelope Houston claims, "the best American critic of the period, and one of the best writers about the cinema in any period."[42] In an era of dreadful motion pictures like *Lost in a Harem* and *Bathing Beauty,* Agee was the one clear voice in the wilderness. His reviews are always probing, intelligent, and interesting, whether he was reviewing Eisenstein's *Ivan the Terrible* or Val Lewton's *The Curse of the Cat People.* Yet, because of the movies he was forced to deal with, Agee's collected film criticism often seems like wasted effort, as though one were reading witty and urbane reviews of illiterate, badly illustrated comic books.

It is difficult to find a consistent critical theory in Agee's uneven film writings, and one does not have to look far for reasons. First of all, Agee was working with a medium that had little more than forty years of tradition. Long considered a genre designed for mass entertainment and momentary titillation, the motion picture had never received truly close scrutiny from aestheticians and theoretical critics. Agee was therefore starting largely from scratch. Secondly, the vast number of atrocious films that Agee was compelled to review made anything like ideal standards impossible. Almost all the films that came off the Hollywood production line between 1940 and 1950 were mediocre; at best, they achieved a high level of mediocrity.

Finally, the necessities of commercial film reviewing—its deadlines, weekly columns, and rapid evaluations—gave Agee little chance to synthesize his disparate thoughts on film-making into any kind of unified whole.

But it would also be false to say that Agee's reviews were impressionistic, devoid of any standards or critical acumen. He seems, rather, to be the only American film critic of his time who was trying to grope his way, however unsuccessfully, toward a coherent aesthetic of the film. He has, at most times, a fugitive vision of what a film *should* be: "Those who think that I am quibbling over detail instead of deploring an ignorance of basic obligations," he says, after deflating several of Hollywood's latest highly touted productions, "should logically think the same if I objected to a performance of a Mozart quartet on a bass ocharina, a kazoo, and a team of Hickman whistles, or pointed out inadequacies in a production of *Coriolanus* which was staged by a particularly art-minded group of fox terriers."[43] At the same time, Agee is willing to accept many motion pictures on their own terms, admiring them for what they are. He is particularly impressed by the productions of Val Lewton, such unpretentious offerings as *The Curse of the Cat People* (according to Agee, "a brave, sensitive, and admirable little psychological melodrama"),[44] *Youth Runs Wild, Isle of the Dead,* and *The Body Snatchers.* Some skeptical viewers of Lewton's productions accused Agee of partiality, some even suspected him of nepotism. But Agee was merely searching for artistry, and he was willing to seek it in unlikely places. His strength as a critic lay in what W. H. Auden calls his "extraordinary wit and felicity,"[45] a profound insight into, coupled with a strong love for, a medium which either directly or indirectly has touched the life of almost every American born in this century.

Agee's film criticism, which Auden ranks with the music critiques of Berlioz and Shaw, more often brings to mind the prefaces of Henry James. Just as James's *The Art of the Novel* adds up, according to R. P. Blackmur, "to a fairly exhaustive reference book on the technical aspects of the art of fiction,"[46] so *Agee on Film* adds up to a similar kind of reference book on the art of the film. "To criticise," James once wrote, "is to appreciate, to appropriate, to take intellectual possession, to establish in fine a relation with the criticised thing and make it one's own."[47] If there is any critical statement lying behind *Agee on Film,* it would have to be something like the preceding one from James. If Agee's criticism fails in any way, it is because much of it, as Pechter points out, "illuminates the mind of the critic rather than the work criticised. After all, movies like *And the Angels Sing, Bride by Mistake,* or *Roger Touhy, Gangster* have to be less important than what any sensitive and intelligent person can say about them."[48]

If it was Agee's task to illuminate the art of the film, it is a commentator's task to illuminate Agee. But when dealing with such a large and random collection of essays as those in *Agee on Film,* it is a difficult task to perform. Many of the essays are contradictory, hastily conceived, and sketchy. Others dwell on topical events (World War II, for example) or on matters of morality rather than aesthetics. To analyze each article fully is an impossible task and, moreover, is beyond the purposes of this chapter. A complete account of Agee's contribution to film criticism requires another full-length book. What a commentator can do, however, is to indicate by example and brief discussion the essential content of the entire volume of essays. The following then is an outline of Agee's general thinking about the art of the film, its purposes, functions, and technical workings.

THE PURPOSE OF A MOTION PICTURE.   The main function of a film, according to Agee, is to involve

the viewer in experiences which he is unlikely to
have at first hand. These "second-hand" experiences,
visually depicted, are more vivid than the written
word, broader in scope than the experiences of the
restricted dramatic stage. Agee, concerned with
the more deeply felt experiences and sufferings of
European nations, believed such second-hand
experiences to be of utmost importance to American
audiences. "Since it is beyond our power to involve
ourselves as deeply in experience as the people of Russia,
England, China, Germany, Japan," Agee stated, "we
have to make up the difference as well as we can at second
hand. Granting that knowledge at second hand, taken
at a comfortable distance, is of itself choked with new and
terrible liabilities, I believe nevertheless that much
could be done to combat and reduce those liabilities, and
that second-hand knowledge is at least less dangerous
than no knowledge at all. And I think it is obvious that in
imparting it, moving pictures could be matchlessly
useful."[49]

THE MORALITY OF FILMS.   It is obvious that if
motion pictures have this pragmatic and social function
of involving us in second-hand experiences, the
successful motion picture must be that which is true
to its vision of experience. The motion picture has,
in Agee's opinion, a certain moral obligation to
transcribe experience as accurately and honestly as
possible. Any motion picture that fails to do so is
open to criticism from both an aesthetic and a moral
viewpoint. Agee was particularly upset, during the
war years, about the numerous "atrocity" pictures like
Darryl Zanuck's *The Purple Heart* which were
coming from Hollywood's super-patriots. Agee admittedly
felt "extremely queasy watching fiction—especially
persuasive fiction—which pretends to clarify facts that
are not clear, and may never become so. Conditioned

by such amphibious and ambiguous semi-information, we are still more likely than otherwise to do things to defeated enemies which, both morally and materially, will finally damage us more deeply even than them."[50] He sees all of these films as "an ordered and successful effort to condition the people of this country against interfering with, or even questioning, an extremely hard peace against the people of Germany."[51] Clearly shirking their moral and social responsibility to reveal *all* the facts (including all the ambiguities), motion picture producers were offering to the public sensationalism, not true "second-hand" experience, and their motion pictures were open to condemnation on moral grounds.

GOOD AND BAD FILMS.   The best films, according to Agee, were—as I have previously pointed out—what he termed "fiction films," i.e., motion pictures derived from works of fiction. Here the material was clearly discernible, the experience already plotted and awaiting proper translation into visual terms. There is a sense, George Bluestone tells us in *Novels into Film*, "in which a careful film adaptation goes to the original not as a finished work (though this tends to be less true of the classics), but as a kind of raw material, much as the novelist approached *his* experience."[52] Just as the fiction writer's impulse comes from experience, so does the film maker's impulse come from fiction, Agee believed.

Although Agee thought that the potential of the fiction film was greater than any other kind, he did not find that the production of a fiction film was automatically successful. He was disappointed, for example, with the screen version of Graham Greene's *Confidential Agent*. The novel seemed to lend itself to screen adaptation; according to Agee, "Greene achieves in print what more naturally belongs in films, and in a sense does not write novels at all, but verbal movies."[53] But somehow the movie failed in "pace, atmosphere, and visual brilliance," causing Agee to conclude that Greene "may have proved that certain kinds of movies anyhow are better on the page than they can ever be on the screen."[54] Agee's *Noa Noa* further supports this. Still, the fiction film, Agee was convinced, has the greatest potential for success, and we recall that almost all of Agee's own scripts were of this kind.

The movies with the slimmest chance of success, in Agee's opinion, were the "serious" or "idea" films. Agee's review of Zanuck's *Wilson* best reveals the reviewer's thoughts on Hollywood's attempts at profundity. "None of the ideas used in *Wilson*," Agee believed, "is expressed in any better than primer fashion. Anyone who cares to can still get twice as much out of a newspaper and a dozen times as much out of even a mediocre book, so far as ideas are concerned."[55] In order to make ideas visually stimulating, the motion picture must, out of necessity, simplify them (usually to the point of childishness) and, as Agee puts it, "through the desire to sell and ingratiate," it must make ideas acceptable to a tremendously diverse audience. A successful "idea" film, Agee implies, is therefore an impossibility.

As for the most obvious "bad" pictures, Agee regards them with a kind of mock tolerance. "I don't feel that most bad pictures are 'bad enough to be funny'; they are just bad enough to be fascinating, not to say depressing as hell," he claimed.[56] Many of the films he felt compelled to review were so rotten that they defeat any attempt at intelligent commentary: "I would like to be able to make *The Affairs of Susan* sound half as bad as it is, but I know when I'm licked."[57] Others are tolerable: *Three Strangers* is "one of the few recent movies you don't feel rather ashamed about, next morning."[58] Some are interesting because of their attempts, however feeble, to try something new: *The Story of G. I. Joe* is "the first great triumph in the effort to combine 'fiction' and 'documentary' film."[59] But in general, Agee suffered through perhaps the lowest ebb of Hollywood production and sincerely believed that the "whole business has been dying here, ten years or more. Last year, it seems to me, was the all-time low—so far."[60] He prophetically claimed that in "another fifty years—or ten, I am willing to bet—moving pictures will no longer be the central medium. Radio will have taken their place; television very likely, will have taken the place of both."[61]

THE VERBAL AND VISUAL ELEMENT IN FILMS. The obvious essence of a motion picture, as Agee recognized, is motion. A movie must stand or fall on its visual achievement, although Agee believed that "thanks to the depravities of the latter-day 'style,' most of us have spoiled eyes."[62] Motion picture productions of Shakespeare were exceptions to Agee's rule. He found, for example, that the great glory of Olivier's *Henry V* was the language; here was a case in which the language, he believed, clearly overshadowed the visual. But this was a rarity. Agee's concept of a successful motion picture was one like Chaplin's *Monsieur Verdoux,* in which "a munificent complex of characters, ideas, milieux, and tributary styles and tones" was handled with "perfect visual wit and expressiveness and with an all but unblemished grace, force and economy."[63]

THE CAMERA.   In the motion picture, the camera is the essential tool of motion. Agee compared good camera work to the "clean-water physical absoluteness of Tolstoy's writing."[64] The progression of each shot and each group of shots, he believed, should contain "emotion, atmosphere, observation, and psychological weight"[65]—all qualities which Agee readily admitted were missing from the majority of Hollywood productions. The camera's function was to capture surface detail without "dramatizing, prearrangement, or sentimentalization."[66] Any attempt to manipulate the

camera "gets in the way of the high honest average
chance for magnificence which any face or machine or light
or terrain possesses, left to its own devices."[67] And
finally, "if you can invent something worth watching,
the camera should hold still and clear, so that you
can watch it."[68]

CUTTING AND TRANSITIONS.   Just as important as the
camera work of a motion picture is the film cutting. It is
here that the movement, the pace, the rhythm of the
movie either fails or succeeds. The average film, Agee said,
moved "in great blotches of ill-punctuated gabble, filled
with uh's, ah's, and as-I-was-sayings"; films should move
"in clear, resonant sentences, which construct irreducible
paragraphs" and should develop "at discreet intervals . . .
small fine poems."[69] The power and honesty of screen
images lie "in juxtaposition and careful series, in rhythm,
and in a rhythmic and spatial whole."[70] Effective
transitions, obtained by effective cutting, achieve a kind of
"climactic release of energy."[71] But again, Agee sadly
admits that the transitions of most Hollywood efforts are
"diffuse, generalized, and conventional."[72]

MOVIE MUSIC AND TECHNICOLOR.   Music should be
used in a motion picture only when it has to be; when
and where it should be used varies, of course, with each
motion picture. Generally, Agee's feelings about
movie music are contained in a review for the *Nation*
dated May 26, 1945:

> Music can be well used in movies. It was wonderfully used
> in Dovzhenko's *Frontier,* for instance; for another kind
> I like the naive, excitable, perfectly appropriate score of the
> soundtracked version of *The Birth of a Nation;* and
> indeed I think the greatest possibilities have hardly yet
> been touched. But music is just as damaging to nearly
> all fiction films as to nearly all fact films, as it is generally
> used in both today. Its ability to bind together a succession

of images, or to make transitions between blocks of them—not to mention "transitional" and "special-effect" and "montage" passages—inevitably makes for laziness or for slackened imagination in making the images and setting them in order, and in watching them. Still worse, it weakens the emotional imagination both of maker and onlooker, and makes it virtually impossible to communicate or receive ideas. It sells too cheaply and far too sensually all the things it is the business of the screen itself to present. The rough equivalent might be a poet who could dare to read aloud from his own work only if the lights were dimmed and some Debussy was on, very low.[73]

Agee's feelings about the use of color are even more general, although he firmly believed that it had "a great aesthetic future in films."[74] Color is mainly effective, he thought, in costume pieces and musical comedies; too often, in other kinds of films, it becomes "the rankest kind of magazine-illustration and postcard art."[75]

EFFECTIVENESS OF THE WHOLE PRODUCTION. To be truly effective, the motion picture must bring all of these previously mentioned elements together into a coherent whole, and they must be brought together unaffectedly. For example, *The Ox-Bow Incident,* a widely ballyhooed Hollywood offering, disappointed Agee even though he found it "one of the best and most interesting pictures" he had seen in a long time.[76] His disappointment came from the "stiff over-consciousness" that made the whole production "a mosaic of over-appreciated effects which continually robbed nature of its own warmth and energy."[77] In *The Ox-Bow Incident,* "artifice and nature got jammed in such a way as to give a sort of double focus, like off-printing in a comic strip."[78] A motion picture, Agee claims time and again, must unroll naturally and unaffectedly; it must wear its artistry lightly and unpretentiously.

THE DIRECTOR.   The key to the effective production
of a motion picture is the director. To Agee, the
director was the deity behind the entire production,
the father-progenitor of the film. One has only to
glance at some of the early letters to Father Flye to
discover that Agee was always, even during his youth,
taken with directing and directors. His later essays
on Griffith and Huston are merely the mature verbalization
of a kind of hero-worship which Agee had all of his life.
The director was, to Agee, the equivalent of a
symphony conductor, who "selects and blends his
instruments" to achieve aesthetic results.[79] Agee's
directorial trinity consisted of Eisenstein, Griffith,
and Huston, and each "conducted" in a different
manner. Eisenstein, for example, was "interested in finding
out how little a movie can be made to move and yet
move at all, and in giving each movement legendary
grandeur."[80] Griffith's greatness lay in his "power to create
permanent images. All through his work there are
images which are as impossible to forget, once you have
seen them, as some of the grandest and simplest passages
in music or poetry."[81] John Huston's work "has a
unique tension and vitality because the maximum of all
contributing creative energies converge at the one
moment that counts most in a movie—the continuing
moment of committing the story to film. At his best he
makes the story tell itself, makes it seem to happen for the
first and last time at the moment of recording."[82] If
there is, or ever will be, an ideal director, he combines, in
Agee's opinion, the qualities of these three men.

The above may give the reader some idea of the general
pattern of Agee's thinking about the film. Surprisingly,
he mentions little of the matters that one might imagine
he thought deeply about. The relationship of the writer to
the cinema, for example, is seldom mentioned. Agee,
I think, felt himself too much of a "pro," a writer who

could turn a professional hand to any medium, to mouth the coffee-house clichés of the commercial writer who agonizes over the "prostitution of his talent." Besides, he loved the medium of the film too well to treat it unkindly. In general, his thoughts about the artist-film relationship are summarized in a review dated March 2, 1946:

> Anyone who wants to make creatively interesting movies in this country today gets stuck in one of three, or at outside four, ways, all of them too familiar to require more than mention. If he works in Hollywood, it is unlikely that he will get more than a fraction of his best ability on to the screen; and that is not to mention the liability of resignation to compromise, and of self-deceit. If he works on his own, he is unlikely to get his films distributed or even sporadically shown; and that is not to mention either the difficulty of getting the money and equipment to make the movies or the liability of self-deceit in the direction of arrogance and artiness—the loss of, and contempt for, audience, which can be just as corrupting as its nominal opposite. If, on the other hand, the would-be artist goes abroad to work, he is likely to find, in future, that the advantages are not so clear by a good deal as they were in the past; and unless he is a very specialized—and perhaps also a very limited—artist indeed, he is certain to suffer as profoundly by a change of country as he would, if he were a writer, by a change of language. The fourth possibility is paralysis, or resignation to the practice of some more feasible art. Either of these is perhaps preferable to literary suicide, but not practically so as far as the movie artist and the movie art are concerned.[83]

This is as close to agonizing as Agee ever gets, although the entire statement has a pragmatic ring to it. This is the

way it is for the "movie artist," and any writer who
wishes to become one must grapple with these very real
problems.

Equally surprising are Agee's scant comments on
acting, even though he was passionately interested in acting
and even appeared in his own television play on Lincoln.
He liked best, when he does comment upon them,
those actors whose talents appear natural and unaffected
on the screen. He disliked Bette Davis, for example,
for what he thought were her set mannerisms. In a review
of *The Corn Is Green* he laments that he never saw
Ethel Barrymore play the leading role on stage (Bette
Davis had the film role), for "people tell me that she
would have left me with my tongue hanging out, and by
my own experience of Miss Barrymore I can find no
reason to doubt it. Bette Davis left me with my tongue
in my head, and I hope I can make it a civil one."[84]

SILENT COMEDY.   Finally there is one more area of
Agee's critical thought that certainly merits discussion in
even the most general analysis of his work—silent
comedy. Perhaps the finest article ever written on screen
comedy is Agee's "Comedy's Greatest Era," which
appeared in *Life* magazine, September 3, 1949. The silent
screen comedians, Agee believed, discovered "beauties
of comic motion which are hopelessly beyond reach
of words."[85] Modern screen comedy fails to achieve this
visual poetry. "To put it unkindly," Agee said, "the
only thing wrong with screen comedy today is that it takes
place on a screen which talks."[86] Agee begins his
analysis of silent comedy by claiming (perhaps somewhat
tongue-in-cheek) that there are four grades of laughter:

In the language of screen comedians four of the main
grades of laugh are the titter, the yowl, the bellylaugh and
the boffo. The titter is just a titter. The yowl is a

runaway titter. Anyone who has ever had the pleasure knows all about the bellylaugh. The boffo is the laugh that kills. An ideally good gag, perfectly constructed and played, would bring the victim up this ladder of laughs by cruelly controlled degrees to the top rung, and would then proceed to wobble, shake, wave and brandish the ladder until he groaned for mercy. Then, after the shortest possible time out for recuperation, he would feel the first wicked tickling of the comedian's whip once more and start up a new ladder.[87]

It was the art of the silent screen comedians to achieve this ladder of laughs, "to be as funny as possible physically, without the help or hindrance of words."[88] The greatest silent comedian, in Agee's opinion (as well as almost everybody's), was Charlie Chaplin. It seems unlikely, Agee claimed, "that any dancer or actor can ever have excelled him in eloquence, variety or poignancy of motion."[89] Chaplin's greatness, and the greatness of his entire generation of comedians, lay in four contributions to comedy technique: milking, inflection, maintaining the comic line, and delaying the ultrapredictable. Milking, as Agee defines it, is the art of building up a gag—or "how to get still funnier."[90] Inflection is "the perfect, changeful shading of [the comedian's] physical and emotional attitudes toward the gag."[91] Maintaining the comic line is a matter of sustaining the gag once it gets going. One should never achieve "a too-big laugh, then a letdown," or strive for "a laugh which is out of key or irrelevant."[92] Finally, delaying the ultrapredictable is explained by Agee in his description of the following scene from a Harold Lloyd movie:

A proper delaying of the ultrapredictable can of course be just as funny as a properly timed explosion of the

unexpected. As Lloyd approaches the end of his horrible
hegira up the side of the building in *Safety Last,* it becomes
clear to the audience, but not to him, that if he raises
his head another couple of inches he is going to get
murderously conked by one of the four arms of a revolving
wind gauge. He delays the evil moment almost interminably,
with one distraction and another, and every delay is a
suspense-tightening laugh; he also gets his foot nicely
entangled in a rope, so that when he does get hit,
the payoff of one gag sends him careening head downward
through the abyss into another.[93]

All of these comic techniques must again come together
with naturalness and unpretentiousness, qualities which
Agee constantly stresses. "The early silent comedians," he
states, "never strove for or consciously thought of
anything which could be called artistic 'form,' but they
achieved it."[94]

No analysis can convey the essential qualities of Agee's
reviews, their wit, their charm, their annihilating
thrusts at Hollywood pomposity. It is certain, as Pechter
claims, that "Agee could never have imagined the
possibility of his criticism being collected in a single
volume under so simple, yet so imposing a title. He wrote
for the moment, to direct his audience to films of merit
and rouse its anger at every cheap failure."[95] One can only
hope that new generations of viewers, interested in
the film and passing evenings with late television movies,
will again be directed by Agee's acute commentary.

fulfillment

vi

*I have a fuzzy, very middle-class,
and in a bad sense of the word,
Christian mind, and a very clouded
sensibility.*
—*Agee*, Letters to Father Flye

There are many immediate problems
that threaten to obscure a true evaluation of James Agee,
a writer whom we are still painfully close to. He is,
first of all, essentially a Romantic writer in an age that
repudiates Romanticism, and his writings exhibit a
preoccupation with self, a spontaneity of emotion, and a
fascination with death, the macabre, melancholy, and
childhood. Discussions of Agee center around his
wasteful life, his excesses, and his "sensibility" (discussions
of his sensibility have become almost a cabala). He
is criticized for having failed to objectify his experiences
in writing, for being too "autobiographical." Most of
all, he is dismissed as a promising writer who was corrupted
by commercial pursuits and by Hollywood. W. M.
Frohock speculates sadly on what Agee "could have left
behind if his great gift had not been channeled off in
other directions" and insists that Agee would have had his
footnote in histories of fiction if he had written "what
was expected of him instead of what he most wanted to
write."[1] Similarly, Dwight Macdonald claims that,

129

although Agee was the most gifted writer of his generation and one who might have done major work, he "didn't do it, or not much of it."[2]

The question of whether or not Agee was corrupted by his commercial ventures is a futile one to pursue. Essentially it is a problem for the sociologist, not for the literary critic, for it serves only to obscure Agee's actual accomplishments. One must recall that many a comfortable writer has devoted his life to full-time writing, yet has failed to do major work. Others have worked under considerable hardships (Kafka and Joyce) or have yielded to a seductive, materialistic society (Scott Fitzgerald), yet have produced literary masterpieces. That they might have produced more under more favorable circumstances is sheer speculation. Is it, perhaps, that we expect too much of our writers today? John Updike, writing about Agee, believes that we do:

> A fever of self-importance is upon American writing. Popular expectations of what literature should provide have risen so high that failure is the only possible success, and pained incapacity the only acceptable proof of sincerity. When ever in prose has slovenliness been so esteemed, ineptitude so cherished? In the present apocalyptic atmosphere, the loudest sinner is most likely to be saved; Fitzgerald's crack-up is his ticket to Heaven, Salinger's silence his claim to our devotion. The study of literature threatens to become a kind of paleontology of failure, and criticism a supercilious psychoanalysis of authors. I resist Agee's canonization by these unearthly standards. Authors should be honored only for their works. If Agee is to be remembered, it should be for his few, uneven, hard-won successes. The author of *Let Us Now Praise Famous Men* and *A Death in the Family* owes no apology to posterity.[3]

It seems clear, therefore, that any evalution of James Agee must concern itself with what he did, not with what he might have done. Only by clearly looking at Agee's "few, uneven, hard-won successes" can we determine the extent of his accomplishments.

If there is any pattern to the entire body of Agee's work, it lies in his cinematic vision of experience. Each genre that Agee worked in—poetry, reportage, social doctrine, and fiction—was a stage toward the achievement of a more complex vision of reality which he unsuccessfully sought to express in the motion picture. It is difficult to trace this development biographically, for at no time does Agee express such a conscious pursuit. He was always passionately concerned with the motion picture, however, and, as Macdonald states, his best writing "has a cinematic flow and immediacy."[4]

A close examination of Agee's writings reveals two basic reasons why his work moved increasingly closer to a kind of cinematic reality. The first reason is an aesthetic one, the belief that words "cannot embody; they can only describe."[5] Agee's preoccupation with bringing words as near as possible to "an illusion of embodiment" served only to undermine his faith in words and to enhance the possibilities of the motion picture camera. Agee, according to Macdonald, was always a frustrated movie maker, "for if words cannot embody, pictures can, and without illusion—a picture is an artistic fact in itself, unlike a word."[6] One has only to consider the full implication of the final sonnet in *Permit Me Voyage* to see that Agee may have consciously abandoned his early desire to be a poet:

> My sovereign souls, God grant my sometime brothers,
> I must desert your ways now if I can.
> I followed hard but now forsake all others,

And stand in hope to make myself a man.
This mouth that blabbed so loud with foreign song
I'll shut awhile, or gargle if I sing.[7]

Finding poetry a "foreign song," Agee resolved to shut his
mouth awhile or "gargle" in the more prosaic media
of journalism and fiction. His journalism and fiction, too,
are deeply rooted in the aesthetics of the film: it is
only a short step from the photographic detail, mood, and
vision of *Let Us Now Praise Famous Men* or *A Death
in the Family* to the visual realism of the motion picture.

The second reason that Agee abandoned poetry,
reportage, and fiction lies in his desire for a truly
"democratic" art. Although Agee was, according to Jack
Behar, "a writer who came of age in the thirties, a time
when political factionalism and a sense of impending
revolutionary upheaval, and a gross uncertainty about the
worth of tradition made up the context in which literary
judgments were offered,"[8] it is by no means clear as to
what extent Agee was a "social" writer. "I am a
Communist by sympathy and conviction," he once wrote
in the thirties, and went on to justify his position:

But it does not appear (just for one thing) that Communists
have recognized or in any case made anything serious
of the sure fact that the persistence of what once was
insufficiently described as Pride, a mortal sin, can quite
as coldly and inevitably damage and wreck the human race
as the most total power of "Greed" ever could: and
that socially anyhow, the dangerous form of pride is neither
arrogance nor humility, but its mild, common denominator
form, complacency. . . . Artists, for instance, should be
capable of figuring the situation out to the degree that they
would refuse the social eminence and the high pay
they are given in Soviet Russia. The setting up of an
aristocracy of superior workers is no good sign, either.[9]

Although out of step with the Left, he was not "any more congruous with the Right, Macdonald claims:

> Although he was deeply religious, he had his own kind of religion, one that included irreverence, blasphemy, obscenity, and even Communism (of his own kind). By the late forties, a religio-conservative revival was under way, but Agee felt as out of place as ever. "If my shapeless comments can be of any interest or use," he characteristically began his contribution to a *Partisan Review* symposium on Religion and the Intellectuals, "it will be because the amateur and the amphibian should be represented in such a discussion. By amphibian I mean that I have a religious background and am 'pro-religious'— though not on the whole delighted by this so-called revival—but doubt that I will return to religion." Amateurs don't flourish in an age of specialization, or amphibians in a time when educated armies clash by night.[10]

Neither concerned with the Leftist's sanctification of the Rickettses and Gudgers nor with the middle-class, conservative pietism of the Right, Agee was truly a democratic writer, involved with all classes and all people. More exactly, he was concerned with the "majority" of people (the Follets, for example, are certainly a middle-class family with middle-class values); his vision of them, however, was from a more intellectually aristocratic point-of-view. That he avoids mawkishness in his portrayal of the Follets can be due only to his dissociation from their values; or, more exactly, it is because he sees their values from a broader, more humanitarian vantage point. In one unpublished letter to Dwight Macdonald, Agee mocked every faction of his time—Right and Left, Jew and Gentile, philistine and intellectual. The letter, according to Macdonald, was "calculated to offend the sensibilities of every

right-thinking and wrong-thinking group in the country."[11]
It is precisely this lack of factionalism, class loyalty,
and regional sympathy that drove Agee increasingly further
toward an art form that would transcend all factions,
classes, and regions. In this "democratic" sense, the ideal
art form was the motion picture. It seemed a medium
capable, in theory if not in practice, of artistic achievement;
of appeal to the widest possible audience regardless of
background, status, or sophistication; and of visual
representation of life without the intervening consciousness
of a mind that is constantly making value judgments.
The camera, devoid of prejudice, does not lie (although
its user might).

Agee's entire career, therefore, was a search for form,
for the one medium that would have the impulse
of life itself. In spite of his abandoning one form after
another, all of his work was of high quality. Agee's
writings reveal that he kept his "promise," that he fulfilled
whatever expectation others held for him as a writer,
but he fulfilled it in his own way and in a manner
specifically modern and American. His greatest error, as
Macdonald pointed out, was being "spectacularly
born in the wrong time and place."[12] Macdonald elaborates
this notion:

He was too versatile, for one thing. In art as in industry,
this is an age of specialization. There is a definite if
restricted "place" for poetry; there is even a Pulitzer Prize
for it, and poets of far less capacity than Agee have made
neat, firm little reputations. But his best poetry is written in
prose and is buried in his three books. . . .

The times might have done better by Agee. They could
exploit one or two of his gifts, but they couldn't use him
in toto—there was too much there to fit into any one
compartment. In another sense, American culture was not

structured *enough* for Agee's special needs; it was
over-specialized as to function but amorphous as to values.
He needed definition, limitation, discipline, but he found
no firm tradition, no community of artists and intellectuals
that would canalize his energies. One thinks of D. H.
Lawrence, similar to Agee in his rebellious irrationalism,
who was forced to define his own values and his own special
kind of writing precisely because of the hard, clear,
well-developed cultural tradition he reacted so strongly
against.[13]

In an age of specialization, Agee had unspecialized talents,
a broad interest in all forms of writing. Agee considered
himself a "professional" writer, one who could turn a deft
hand to whatever task lay before him (whenever he
had to state his occupation, Agee merely put down
"writer"), and it is because of this view of himself that
his career became a specifically American and
contemporary one. How, in America, can a writer write?
Unless he turns out masterpiece after masterpiece,
an impossible task that would require super-human talent,
or best-seller after best-seller, in which case one is
no longer an artist, but a commercial purveyor of ephemera
for mass consumption, a writer is forced to practice
his craft in various fields: television, motion pictures,
journals. Only in this way can he practice his profession,
gain needed experience, and make enough money to
subsidize his private and less profitable writing ventures.
Another alternative is to become a teacher-writer
(such as Archibald MacLeish or Karl Shapiro), a
businessman-writer (Wallace Stevens), a lecturer-writer
(Robert Frost), or a politician-writer (Norman
Mailer or Gore Vidal). But any of these alternatives force
a writer into a dual existence, one which Agee was
not capable of pursuing, by temperament, training, or

inclination. What we should not lose sight of is
the fact that Agee worked as a writer, in a continuing
writer's role, and produced high-quality work in whatever
endeavor he turned his hand to. Agee, one must
conclude, took the only direction that a twentieth-century
American, devoted solely to being a "writer," could
possibly take.

A summary of the analyses presented earlier should
sufficiently indicate the quality and direction of Agee's
entire body of work. *Permit Me Voyage* reveals Agee as a
talented but uneven poet. His best poems—"Sunday:
Outskirts of Knoxville, Tenn.," "Rapid Transit," "Ann
Garner," and some of the "Lyrics" and "Sonnets"—are
tightly controlled, intense, emotional, and original.
His worst are artificial and imitative. In general, the poems
are not only the work of a young poet perfecting his
art, they are the work of a mature poet bringing to fruition
a small but exquisite talent. It is conceivable that even
if Agee had not produced any other major work, he would
have been remembered for his poetry alone. Some of
his poems are already becoming anthologized, a sign that
he is being admitted into the contemporary canon,
and a new edition of his poetry is soon to be published.
What prevented Agee from being a greater poet than
he was is his lack of a distinctive voice. Some of his best
lines, like these,

> Life was in death:
> The world rolled black and barren in its mists,
> And life was locked deep in the sheathing snows;
> Then wind and sun and rain came, like a lover,
> Clasping the world in fierce, caressing arms.[14]

have a Miltonic ring, while others—"All the heavens
seemed to slip/And swoop and shuttle, weaving a wild

web/Of gold across the sky"[15]—have an Elizabethan
cadence and imagery. Although some readers have seen his
poems focusing on the Leftist ideals of the thirties,
it is more clear today that the poems avoid factionalism.
Concerned with universal topics, Agee is a conservative,
traditional, and somewhat romantic poet whose
work is often derivative, but always intense and technically
proficient. In short, Agee is an excellent minor poet.

Agee's early talent was much more suited for reportage
than for poetry, and it was natural that this is where
he would turn. All of his journalistic efforts, with the
possible exception of "Six Days at Sea," have little
literary merit and are not worth consideration in Agee's
major canon. *Let Us Now Praise Famous Men,* however,
is a different matter. It is the fruit of a hitherto
thwarted reportorial mind, the supreme achievement of
an artist who combined in a literary work the poet's
vision and the reporter's eye for detail. It is, as Lionel
Trilling has stated, "a great book,"[16] in the mainstream of
American liberal writing and reminiscent of such
works as *Moby Dick, Walden,* and *Leaves of Grass.* It is
also, like these other works, a maimed giant of a
book with long stretches of tedious description and shrill
declamations about the Nobility of Man. Yet it is a
brilliant and lasting book. It accomplishes more than any
other book of its decade simply because it attempts
to say more. Moreover, it is, as Trilling claims, "full of
marvelous writing which gives a kind of hot pleasure
that words can do so much."[17] All told, it is one of Agee's
two supreme achievements.

If about half of Agee's literary reputation will be based
on *Let Us Now Praise Famous Men,* the other half
will be based largely on *A Death in the Family.* It is
difficult, looking backward, to think of a better novel that
has been published in the last two decades. Despite

its incompletion, it has a beautifully controlled structure
and irony, a depth of characterization, and a descriptive
poetry that few novels of our time remotely approach.
It is a complex work, with a compelling humanity and
universality. *A Death in the Family* is easy to sneer at, for
it is peculiarly out of step with its time and it asserts
none of the current attitudes that critics find beguiling.
It has no masculine posturing, no modern *Weltschmerz,*
no fashionable degradation of the human spirit. It
is a simple, strikingly human, humane, and old-fashioned
novel. One can only speculate on its future, but there
is the suspicion that when other, more popular writers have
been objectified by the passage of time, James Agee
and his one quiet novel will rank very high among modern
works of fiction. Such speculation, however, is idle;
A Death in the Family now stands as a successful work of
fiction whose popularity seems to be increasing. The
novel clearly needs no apologies.

Among Agee's minor fiction, *The Morning Watch* and
"A Mother's Tale" deserve recognition. *The Morning
Watch,* although a moving and well-written novel, fails to
achieve the level of quality of *A Death in the Family.*
It is an uneven book, intense, introspective, and sometimes
tedious. As a first novel, nonetheless, it is impressive
and provides an effective introduction to the obsessive
themes found in Agee's other work. "A Mother's Tale" is
a Kafkaesque horror story, a parable of warfare,
human cruelty, and alienation. The story is haunting and
impressive, but its meaning is difficult to puzzle out.
The writer of parables must provide his reader with keys,
in the form of public symbols, which help to unlock
his meaning; Agee may have failed to provide us with
enough of those keys. Finally, one must keep in mind that
more of Agee's minor fiction may be published in the
future. Any present assessment of his contribution as a
fiction writer is subject to change.

Whatever his future in the history of fiction, James Agee will certainly have a prominent place in the history of the cinema. Although the film scripts that he turned out are all literate and entertaining, none of them is especially memorable. *The Quiet One* is the most artistic; *The Night of the Hunter* is the most entertaining; *The African Queen* is the most commercial; and *Noa-Noa* is the most ambitious. But compared with the scripts of Bergman, Fellini, Eisenstein, or even Dudley Nichols, Agee's scripts seem good but not great. It is, instead, as a film critic that Agee achieves the greatness he so earnestly desired for his scripts. There seems to be little doubt among film scholars that Agee was the best reviewer in America during the forties. His reviews are urbane, witty, and perceptive, the work of a man who is passionately concerned with the artistic potential of the film and is deeply disturbed by the contemporary lack of artistry. Taken as a whole, Agee's reviews comprise a textbook on the art of the film, written not with a scholar's interest but with a lover's fondness.

In summary, James Agee is a writer who "kept his promise" in his own way. In the mainstream of American writing, he has made a solid and important contribution to modern literature. During a brief career, he wrote two excellent books, *Let Us Now Praise Famous Men* and *A Death in the Family;* one competent one, *The Morning Watch;* one solid volume of verse; a body of the finest film reviews written during his time; and several minor works of reportage and letters. As a technical innovator, he brought, in W. M. Frohock's opinion, "a technique of script-writing, perhaps the essential technique of script-writing, to the writing of a novel."[18] Furthermore, Agee attempted to rechannel the novel from the contemporary concern with the degenerate and idiosyncratic to the universal concern with the human and humane, and he did so without mawkishness or falsity.

Like all writers, however, he has his faults, and they are
fairly obvious. His poetic prose often sounds artificial
and turns into bad poetry; his endless catalogs, particularly
in *Let Us Now Praise Famous Men,* are often more
tedious than entertaining; and the texture of his work never
reaches the degree of connotation and richness as that
of Joyce, Mann, Proust, or Virginia Woolf. But if his
writings are not poetry, they at least have the spirit of
poetry; if his characters lack the impact of more
tragic modern fictional creations, they are nonetheless
memorable and believable; if the rhetoric occasionally runs
rampant and the symbols sometimes seem contrived,
at least the final result of the rhetoric and symbols is that
they form a successful and meaningful literary
production. All things considered, therefore, James Agee
was one of America's finest writers during the forties
and early fifties.

As a modern writer, Agee has pointed the way (and
it may be a bleak one) for future creative talents.
"America," W. M. Frohock says, "now maintains so many
areas in which a creative talent can find room for
exercise that a writer whose gifts at one time would have
assured us a long series of good fictions is now invited
to divert his energies in a dozen different directions."[19] In
our present electric age, in which, as Marshall McLuhan
states, "the medium is the message," the lineal, sequential
pattern of the written word is only one of many
modes of expression at a writer's disposal. "Today in the
electric age," claims McLuhan, "we feel as free to
invent nonlineal logics as we do to make non-Euclidean
geometries."[20] Radio, television, motion pictures, and
recordings have given the "writer" new realms for
exploration, new ways of making his audience hear and
see, and Agee was one of the first artists to explore
their potential. Furthermore, Agee was an American, "of

a race that matures slowly, if ever."[21] Given the
nature of his society, the age in which he lived, his
irresponsible self-destruction, and what John Updike calls
"his blind, despairing belief in an ideal amateurism,"[22]
it is unlikely that Agee would have produced anything
greater than he did in the media we still consider "literary."
To speculate on the poetry or fiction that he might
have written is to envision James Agee as someone other
than the man he was: a versatile and accomplished
artist whose mind played freely over all possible media of
expression and whose ability with the English language was
exceeded by none of his contemporaries. Truly an
avant-garde artist, Agee was a writer whose career implies
a new direction that American writers may be taking.
"In other words," according to Frohock, "the men who
could be our major novelists may be going . . .
elsewhere."[23] Agee, it seems, was the first to go.

notes

chapter i

1. Randall Jarrell, *Poetry and the Age* (New York, 1953), p. 148.

2. Alfred Kazin, *Contemporaries* (Boston, 1962), p. 185.

3. Robert Phelps, "James Agee," in *Letters of James Agee to Father Flye* (New York, 1962), p. 1; in subsequent notes this book will be cited as *Letters.*

4. Father James Harold Flye, Introduction to *Letters,* p. 11.

5. James Agee, "James Agee: By Himself," *Esquire,* LX (December, 1963), 290.

6. James Agee, *A Death in the Family* (New York, 1957), p. 217.

7. Flye, Introduction, *Letters,* p. 11.

8. Agee, "James Agee: By Himself," p. 149.

9. Agee, *Letters,* p. 18.

10. *Ibid.*

11. *Ibid.,* p. 19.

12. *Ibid.,* p. 37.

13. *Ibid.*

14. *Ibid.,* p. 34.

15. Agee, "James Agee: By Himself," p. 149.

16. Agee, *Letters,* p. 45.

17. *Ibid.,* p. 46.

18. *Ibid.,* p. 47.

LIBRARY ST. MARY'S COLLEGE

19. W. M. Frohock, "James Agee—The Question of Wasted Talent," in *The Novel of Violence in America,* rev. ed. (Boston, 1964), p. 216.

20. *Ibid.*

21. Agee, *Letters,* pp. 54-55.

22. *Ibid.,* p. 56.

23. *Ibid.,* p. 57.

24. *Ibid.,* p. 62. The article is titled "Sheep and Shuttleworths," and it appeared in *Fortune,* VII (January, 1933), 43.

25. The Tennessee Valley story is "The Project Is Important," *Fortune,* VIII (October, 1933), 81; the story about interior decorating is "What D'You Mean, Modern?" *Fortune,* XII (November, 1935), 97; the orchid story is "The U.S. Commercial Orchid," *Fortune,* XII (December, 1935), 108.

26. Richard Oulahan, "A Cult Grew Around a Many-Sided Writer," *Life,* LV (November 1, 1963), 72. Agee's story appeared in *Fortune,* XVI (September, 1937), 117.

27. Agee, *Letters,* p. 122.

28. Frohock, *The Novel of Violence in America,* p. 224.

29. Agee, *Letters,* p. 63.

30. *Ibid.,* pp. 68-69.

31. Agee, "James Agee: By Himself," pp. 149, 289.

32. Dwight Macdonald, *Against the American Grain* (New York, 1965), p. 152.

33. Walker Evans, "James Agee in 1936," in *Let Us Now Praise Famous Men,* by James Agee and Walker Evans (Boston, 1960), p. ix.

34. Agee, "James Agee: By Himself," p. 149.

35. Agee, *Letters,* p. 132.

36. *Ibid.,* p. 152.

37. *Ibid.,* pp. 170-71.

38. *Ibid.,* pp. 215-16.

39. *Ibid.,* p. 213.

40. Oulahan, "A Cult," pp. 69-70.

41. Agee, *Letters,* p. 229.

42. Oulahan, "A Cult," p. 72.

43. Macdonald, *Against the American Grain,* p. 151.

44. *Ibid*

chapter ii

1. Archibald MacLeish, Introduction to *Permit Me Voyage* (New Haven, 1934), p. 7.

2. James Agee and Walker Evans, *Let Us Now Praise Famous Men* (Boston, 1960), p. 238.

3. Dwight Macdonald, *Against the American Grain* (New York, 1965), p. 154.

4. Ezra Pound, *Literary Essays of Ezra Pound,* ed. and intro. T. S. Eliot (Norfolk, Conn., 1954), p. 23.

5. James Agee, "Rapid Transit," *Forum,* XCVII (February, 1937), 115. Reprinted in Louis Untermeyer (ed.), *Modern American Poetry* (New York, 1958), p. 607.

6. Elizabeth Drew (ed.), *Directions in Modern Poetry* (New York, 1940), p. 243.

7. James Agee, "Sunday: Outskirts of Knoxville, Tenn.," *New Masses,* XXIV (September 14, 1937), 22. Reprinted in Drew, *Directions in Modern Poetry,* pp. 243-44.

8. Drew, *Directions in Modern Poetry,* p. 247.

9. Agee, *Letters,* pp. 58-59.

10. Peter Ohlin, *Agee* (New York, 1966), p. 22.

11. All quotations from *Permit Me Voyage* are from the Yale University Press edition, second printing, 1935. Henceforth, page numbers of longer quotations will follow the quotation in parentheses.

12. Agee, *Permit Me Voyage,* pp. 18, 23.

13. Agee, *Letters,* p. 38.

14. *Ibid.,* p. 48.

15. *Ibid.,* p. 56.

chapter iii

1. Alfred Kazin, *Contemporaries* (Boston, 1962), p. 186.

2. Alfred Kazin, *On Native Grounds* (New York, 1956), p. 287.

3. Daniel Aaron, *Writers on the Left* (New York, 1965), p. 404.

4. Walker Evans, "James Agee in 1936," in *Let Us Now Praise Famous Men* by James Agee and Walker Evans (Boston, 1960), p. xi.

5. Richard Oulahan, "A Cult Grew around a Many-Sided Writer," *Life,* LV (November 1, 1963), 72.

6. James Agee, Preface to *Let Us Now Praise Famous Men,* p. xiv.

7. James Baldwin, *Notes of a Native Son* (Boston, 1955), p. 19.

8. Lionel Trilling, "An American Classic," *The Mid-Century,* XVI, no. 16 (September, 1960), 4.

9. *Ibid.*

10. Agee, *Let Us Now Praise Famous Men,* p. 12.

11. *Ibid.,* p. xv.

12. *Ibid.*

13. Trilling, "An American Classic," p. 5

14. *Ibid.*

15. Agee, *Let Us Now Praise Famous Men,* p. 13.

16. *Ibid.,* p. 235.

17. *Ibid.,* p. 242.

18. *Ibid.,* p. 243.

19. *Ibid.*

20. *Ibid.,* pp. xviii, xix.

21. Peter Ohlin finds the structure more like "a Shakespearean five-act drama (as *Julius Caesar*), or a Beethoven symphony (the Fifth)." Whatever the number of parts, the dramatic and musical analogy seems clear. See Ohlin, *Agee* (New York, 1966), p. 58.

22. Agee, *Let Us Now Praise Famous Men,* p. 19.

23. *Ibid.* pp. 470-71.

24. *Ibid.,* p. 11.

25. *Ibid.,* p. 28.

26. *Ibid.,* p. 30.

27. Dwight Macdonald, "Death of a Poet," *New Yorker,* XXXIII (November 16, 1957), 237.

28. Agee, *Let Us Now Praise Famous Men,* p. 105.

29. *Ibid.,* p. 78.

30. *Ibid.,* p. 107.

31. *Ibid.,* p. xx.

32. *Ibid.,* p. 210.

33. *Ibid.,* p. 305.

34. Trilling, *An American Classic,* p. 4.

35. *Ibid.,* p. 7.

36. *Ibid.*

37. Agee, *Let Us Now Praise Famous Men,* p. 289.

38. See Richard Hofstadter, *The Age of Reform* (New York, 1955), pp. 60-93.

39. Richard Chase, *The American Novel and its Tradition* (New York, 1957), pp. 201-202.

40. Agee, *Let Us Now Praise Famous Men*, p. 232.

41. James Agee, *Letters*, p. 186.

42. Frank Norris in Isaac Marcosson, *Adventures in Interviewing* (New York, 1920), p. 235.

43. Agee, *Let Us Now Praise Famous Men*, p. 233.

44. Malcolm Cowley, *The Literary Situation* (New York, 1958), p. 80.

45. Macdonald, "Death of a Poet," p. 239.

chapter iv

1. Joseph Conrad, Preface to *The Nigger of the "Narcissus"* (New York, 1914), pp. vii-x.

2. *Ibid.*, p. x.

3. Henry James, *Partial Portraits* (London, 1888), p. 390.

4. James Agee, *A Death in the Family* (New York, 1957), pp. 80-81.

5. See Richard Oulahan, "A Cult Grew around a Many-Sided Writer," *Life*, LV (November 1, 1963), 72; and Dwight Macdonald, *Against the American Grain* (New York, 1965), p. 151.

6. It was the September, 1937, issue, Vol. XVI, no. 3.

7. James Agee, "Six Days at Sea," *Fortune*, XVI (September, 1937), 117.

8. *Ibid.*

9. *Ibid.*, p. 118.

10. *Ibid.*, p. 119.

11. *Ibid.*, pp. 212, 214.

12. *Ibid.*, p. 216.

13. *Ibid.*, p. 219.

14. *Ibid.*, p. 220.

15. James Agee, "A Mother's Tale" in *Twenty-Three Modern Stories*, ed. Barbara Howes (New York, 1963), p. 16.

16. *Ibid.*, p. 17.

17. *Ibid.*, p. 19.

18. *Ibid.*, p. 23.

19. *Ibid.*

20. Alan Pryce-Jones, Preface to the paperback reprint of *The Morning Watch* (New York, 1966), p. xvii.

21. James Agee, "The Morning Watch" in *Thirteen Great Stories,* ed. Daniel Talbot (New York, 1961), p. 207.

22. *Ibid.,* p. 196.

23. *Ibid.,* p. 199.

24. *Ibid.,* p. 200.

25. *Ibid.,* p. 210.

26. *Ibid.,* p. 225.

27. *Ibid.,* p. 246.

28. *Ibid.,* p. 248.

29. *Ibid.*

30. *Ibid.,* p. 250.

31. *Ibid.,* p. 255.

32. *Ibid.,* p. 243.

33. Macdonald, *Against the American Grain,* p. 147.

34. Agee, *A Death in the Family,* p. 144.

35. *Ibid.,* p. 176.

36. *Ibid.,* p. 134.

37. *Ibid.,* pp. 82-83.

38. *Ibid.,* p. 229.

39. *Ibid.,* p. 234.

40. *Ibid.,* p. 239.

41. *Ibid.,* p. 213.

42. See, for example, Macdonald, *Against the American Grain,* p. 145.

43. Agee, *A Death in the Family,* p. 56.

44. *Ibid.,* pp. 308-309.

45. *Ibid.,* p. 311.

46. *Ibid.,* p. 316.

47. *Ibid.,* pp. 334-35.

48. *Ibid.,* p. 335.

49. *Ibid.,* p. 19.

50. *Ibid.,* p. 303.

51. *Ibid.,* p. 305.

52. *Ibid.,* p. 143.

53. *Ibid.,* p. 142.

54. *Ibid.,* p. 195.

55. *Ibid.,* p. 188.

56. Ashley Montagu, "The Natural Superiority of Women," *Saturday Review,* XXXV (March 1, 1952), 28.

57. Agee, *A Death in the Family,* p. 174.

58. *Ibid.,* p. 207.

59. *Ibid.,* p. 153.

60. *Ibid.,* p. 338.

61. *Ibid.,* p. 61.
62. *Ibid.,* p. 68.
63. *Ibid.*
64. *Ibid.,* p. 70.
65. *Ibid.,* p. 296.
66. *Ibid.,* p. 297.
67. *Ibid.,* p. 337.
68. Jack Behar, *James Agee: The World of His Work,* unpublished doctoral dissertation, Ohio State University, 1963, p. 203.
69. Agee, *A Death in the Family,* p. 94.
70. See the record jacket of Samuel Barber's *Knoxville: Summer of 1915,* Columbia Records, ML 5843.
71. Agee, *A Death in the Family,* pp. 3-5.
72. *Ibid.,* p. 84.
73. *Ibid.*
74. *Ibid.,* p. 219.
75. *Ibid.,* p. 37.
76. James Agee and Walker Evans, *Let Us Now Praise Famous Men* (Boston, 1960), p. 56.

chapter v

1. James Agee and Walker Evans, *Let Us Now Praise Famous Men* (Boston, 1960), p. 236.
2. *Ibid.,* p. 234.
3. Rudolf Arnheim, "A Bird's-Eye View of Film," remarks delivered at the second performance of Moving Images, a film series at the University of Virginia, November 18, 1961.
4. Lionel Trilling, "An American Classic," *The Mid-Century,* XVI, no. 16 (September, 1960), 6.
5. Arnheim, "A Bird's-Eye View of Film."
6. Agee, *Let Us Now Praise Famous Men,* p. 356.
7. *Ibid.,* p. 236.
8. *Ibid.*
9. *Ibid.*
10. *Ibid.,* p. 244.
11. *Ibid.,* p. 56.
12. *Ibid.,* p. 187.
13. *Ibid.,* pp. 237-38.
14. *Ibid.,* p. 11.
15. Marshall McLuhan, *Understanding Media: The Extensions of Man* (New York, 1966), p. 249.

16. James Agee, *Agee on Film,* I (New York, 1958), p. 136.

17. See Dwight Macdonald, "Masscult & Midcult," in *Against the American Grain* (New York, 1965), pp. 3-75.

18. See Clement Greenberg, "Avant-Garde and Kitsch," in *Mass Culture: The Popular Arts in America,* eds. Bernard Rosenberg and David Manning White (Glencoe, Ill., 1957), pp. 98-107.

19. Macdonald, *Against the American Grain,* p. 54.

20. See W. H. Auden, "A Letter to the Editors of *The Nation,*" reprinted in *Agee on Film,* I, p. i.

21. Agee. *Agee on Film,* I, 66. For an excellent discussion of the fiction-film relationship see George Bluestone, *Novels into Film* (Baltimore, 1957).

22. Agee, *Agee on Film,* II (New York, 1960), p. 96.

23. William S. Pechter, "On Agee on Film," *Sight and Sound,* XXXIII (Summer, 1964), 152.

24. Agee, *Agee on Film,* II, p. 381.

25. *Ibid.,* p. 475.

26. *Ibid.,* p. 487.

27. Macdonald, *Against the American Grain,* p. 151.

28. Agee, *Agee on Film,* II, p. 311.

29. Pechter, "On Agee on Film," pp. 152-53.

30. Agee, *Agee on Film,* II, p. 3.

31. Pechter, "On Agee on Film," p. 151.

32. Agee, *Agee on Film,* II, p. 6.

33. *Ibid.,* p. 23.

34. *Ibid.,* p. 60.

35. *Ibid.,* p. 44.

36. *Ibid.,* p. 146.

37. *Ibid.,* p. 138.

38. Agee, *Letters,* pp. 215-16.

39. Agee, *Agee on Film,* II, p. 139.

40. Pechter, "On Agee on Film," p. 153.

41. Agee, *Agee on Film,* I, p. 22.

42. Penelope Houston, *The Contemporary Cinema* (Baltimore, 1963), p. 46.

43. Agee, *Agee on Film,* I, p. 26.

44. *Ibid.,* p. 85.

45. Auden, "A Letter to the Editors of *The Nation,*" p. i.

46. R. P. Blackmur, Introduction to Henry James, *The Art of the Novel* (New York, 1960), p. viii.

47. James, *The Art of the Novel,* p. 155.

48. Pechter, "On Agee on Film," p. 148.
49. Agee, *Agee on Film*, I, p. 56.
50. *Ibid.*, p. 80.
51. *Ibid.*, p. 161.
52. Bluestone, *Novels into Film*, p. 90.
53. Agee, *Agee on Film*, I, p. 179.
54. *Ibid.*
55. *Ibid.*, p. 111.
56. *Ibid.*, p. 61.
57. *Ibid.*, p. 153.
58. *Ibid.*, p. 193.
59. *Ibid.*, p. 173.
60. *Ibid.*, p. 67.
61. *Ibid.*, p. 65.
62. *Ibid.*, p. 255.
63. *Ibid.*, p. 254.
64. *Ibid.*, p. 149.
65. *Ibid.*, p. 150.
66. *Ibid.*, p. 33.
67. *Ibid.*
68. *Ibid.*, p. 255.
69. *Ibid.*, p. 34.
70. *Ibid.*
71. *Ibid.*, p. 174.
72. *Ibid.*
73. *Ibid.*, p. 164.
74. *Ibid.*, p. 48.
75. *Ibid.*
76. *Ibid.*, p. 44.
77. *Ibid.*
78. *Ibid.*
79. *Ibid.*, p. 210.
80. *Ibid.*, p. 248.
81. *Ibid.*, p. 313.
82. *Ibid.*, p. 326.
83. *Ibid.*, p. 190.
84. *Ibid.*, p. 157.
85. *Ibid.*, p. 3.
86. *Ibid.*, p. 4.
87. *Ibid.*, p. 2.
88. *Ibid.*, p. 3.
89. *Ibid.*, p. 9.
90. *Ibid.*, p. 18.

91. *Ibid.*, p. 9.

92. *Ibid.*

93. *Ibid.*, pp. 11-12.

94. *Ibid.*, p. 6.

95. Pechter, "On Agee on Film," p. 151.

chapter vi

1. W. M. Frohock, *The Novel of Violence in America* (Boston, 1964), p. 224.

2. Dwight Macdonald, *Against the American Grain* (New York, 1965), p. 144.

3. John Updike, "No Use Talking," *New Republic,* CXLVII (August 13, 1962), 23.

4. Macdonald, *Against the American Grain,* p. 153.

5. James Agee and Walker Evans, *Let Us Now Praise Famous Men* (Boston, 1960), p. 238.

6. Macdonald, *Against the American Grain,* p. 155.

7. James Agee, *Permit Me Voyage* (New Haven, 1934), p. 58.

8. Jack Behar, *James Agee: The World of His Work,* unpublished doctoral dissertation, Ohio State University, 1963, p. 21.

9. Quoted in Macdonald, *Against the American Grain,* p. 155.

10. *Ibid.*, p. 156.

11. *Ibid.*, pp. 162-63.

12. *Ibid.*, p. 153.

13. *Ibid.*, pp. 153-54.

14. Agee, *Permit Me Voyage,* p. 31.

15. *Ibid.*, p. 33.

16. Lionel Trilling, "An American Classic," *The Mid-Century,* XVI, no. 16 (September, 1960), 4.

17. *Ibid.*, p. 7.

18. Frohock, *The Novel of Violence in America,* p. 228.

19. *Ibid.*, p. 212.

20. Marshall McLuhan, *Understanding Media: The Extensions of Man* (New York, 1966), p. 88.

21. Macdonald, *Against the American Grain,* p. 159.

22. Updike, "No Use Talking," p. 23.

23. Frohock, *The Novel of Violence in America,* p. 230.

bibliography*

primary sources

I. James Agee's Fiction

"Minerva Farmer," *Phillips Exeter Monthly*, XXX (November, 1925), 39-42.

"The Bell Tower of Amiens," *Phillips Exeter Monthly*, XXX (December, 1925), 48-51.

"The Scar," *Phillips Exeter Monthly*, XXX (January, 1926), 77-78.

"The Circle," *Phillips Exeter Monthly*, XXX (April, 1926), 143-51.

"Phogias and Meion," *Phillips Exeter Monthly*, XXX (May, 1926), 167-71.

"Revival," *Phillips Exeter Monthly*, XXX (May, 1926), 181.

"Jenkinsville I," *Phillips Exeter Monthly*, XXXI (December, 1926), 71-72.

"Jenkinsville II," *Phillips Exeter Monthly*, XXXI (January, 1927), 81-82.

"Knoxton High," *Phillips Exeter Monthly*, XXXI (April, 1927), 161-66.

"Between Trains," *Phillips Exeter Monthly*, XXXI (May, 1927), 171-73.

* I wish to acknowledge the usefulness of Miss Genevieve Fabre's bibliography (*Bulletin of Bibliography*, 24 [1965] 7: 145–58, 163–66) in preparing the bibliography for this book.

"Chivalry—An Allegory," *Phillips Exeter Monthly*, XXXII (November, 1927), 25-40.

"Bound for the Promised Land," *Phillips Exeter Monthly*, XXXII (January, 1928), 85-88.

"Mrs. Bruce and the Spider," *Phillips Exeter Monthly*, XXXII (February, 1928), 113.

"A Sentimental Journey," *Phillips Exeter Monthly*, XXXII (March, 1928), 133-37.

"Sacre du Printemps," *Phillips Exeter Monthly*, XXXII (April, 1928), 158-60.

"A Walk before Mass," *Harvard Advocate*, CXVI (Christmas, 1929), 18-20.

"Boys Will Be Brutes," *Harvard Advocate*, CXVI (April, 1930), 29-33.

"Near the Tracks," *Harvard Advocate*, CXVI (June, 1930), 9-20.

"Death in The Desert," *Harvard Advocate*, CXVII (October, 1930), 16-24.

"You, Andrew Volstead," *Harvard Advocate*, CXVII (March, 1931), 22-29.

"They That Sow in Sorrow Shall Reap," *Harvard Advocate*, CXVII (May, 1931), 9-23.

"A parody of *Time*" number, *Harvard Advocate*, CXVIII (March, 1932), p. 1 to end.

"Knoxville: Summer of 1915," *Partisan Review*, V (August–September, 1938), 22-25. Later published as a prologue to *A Death in the Family* (1957).

"The Morning Watch," *Botteghe Oscure*, VI (1950), 339-409. Also in *Partisan Review*, XVIII (March, 1951), 137-66, 206-31.

The Morning Watch. Boston, Houghton Mifflin, 1951. Reprinted in Daniel Talbot (ed.), *Thirteen Great Stories*. New York, Dell Laurel Edition, 1961, pp. 195-256.

"A Mother's Tale," *Harper's Bazaar* (July, 1952), pp. 66-68, 102-15. Reprinted in Barbara Howes (ed.), *Twenty-Three Modern Stories*. New York, Vintage Books, 1963, pp. 3-25.

"Death in the Family—A Section," *Harper's Bazaar* (July, 1956), pp. 40 ff.

"The Waiting," *New Yorker*, XXXIII (October 5, 1957), 41-62. Incorporated in *A Death in the Family* (1957).

"Rufus," *New Yorker*, XXXIII (November 2, 1957), 36-41.

A Death in the Family. New York, McDowell & Obolensky, 1957.

II.   *James Agee's Poetry*

"Ebb Tide," *Phillips Exeter Monthly,* XXX (November, 1925), 27.

"In Preparation," *Phillips Exeter Monthly,* XXX (November, 1925), 27.

"La Fille aux Cheveux de Lin," *Phillips Exeter Monthly,* XXX (January, 1926), 68.

"China," *Phillips Exeter Monthly,* XXX (January, 1926), 79.

"Beauvais," *Phillips Exeter Monthly,* XXX (May, 1926), 177.

"Widow," *Phillips Exeter Monthly,* XXX (May, 1926), 180.

"Water," *Phillips Exeter Monthly,* XXXI (February, 1927), 96.

"Orbs Terrae," *Phillips Exeter Monthly,* XXXI (May, 1927), 188.

"Menaicas," *Phillips Exeter Monthly,* XXXII (December, 1927), 59-65.

"Ann Garner," *Phillips Exeter Monthly,* XXXII (May, 1928), 177-86.

"Ann Garner" (new version), *Hound and Horn,* II (Spring, 1929), 223-35.

"To Lydia," *Harvard Advocate,* CXV (April, 1929), 33.

"Apotheosis," *Harvard Advocate,* CXV (June, 1929), 21.

"The Storm," *Harvard Advocate,* CXVI (December, 1929), 15.

"The Shadow," *Harvard Advocate,* CXVI (February, 1930), 17.

"A Lovers' Dialogue," *Harvard Advocate,* CXVI (February, 1930), 29.

"The Randez Vous," *Harvard Advocate,* CXVI (March, 1930), 31.

"Good Friday," *Harvard Advocate,* CXVI (April, 1930), 27.

"Resume," *Harvard Advocate,* CXVI (June, 1930), 22.

"Sonnet: Death Never Swoops Us Around . . . ," *Harvard Advocate,* CXVI (Commencement, 1930), 19.

"Sonnet: I Have Been Fashioned on a Chain of Flesh . . . ," *Harvard Advocate,* CXVII (Christmas, 1930), 22.

"Description of Elysium—with Reservations," *Harvard Advocate,* CXIII (March, 1931), 18.

"The Truce," *Harvard Advocate,* CXVII (May, 1931), 58-59.

"Resolution," *Harvard Advocate,* CXVII (May, 1931), 77.

"A Poem of Poets," *Harvard Advocate,* CXVIII (October, 1931), 37.

"Six Sonnets," *Harvard Advocate,* CXVIII (December, 1931), 20-21.

"A Parable of Doors," *Harvard Advocate,* CXVIII (Christmas, 1931), 31.

"The Passionate Poet to His Love," *Harvard Advocate,* CXVII (February, 1932), 21.

"Opening of a Long Poem," *Harvard Advocate,* CXVIII (June, 1932), 12-20.

Agee's Winning Garrison Prize Poems, *Harvard Advocate,* CXIX (April, 1933), 5-9.

"Class Ode," *Harvard Class Album,* 1932, p. 204.

Permit Me Voyage. New Haven, Yale University Press, 1934.

"Lyric" and "A Song," *transition,* No. 24 (June, 1936), p. 7.

"Song With Words," "Two Songs on the Economy of Abundance," "Rapid Transit," and "In Heavy Mind," in Louis Untermeyer (ed.), *Modern American Poetry,* New York, Harcourt, Brace, 1936; also in 1950 edition, pp. 637-41.

"Rapid Transit," *Forum,* XCVII (February, 1937), 115. Reprinted in Louis Untermeyer (ed.), *Modern American Poetry.* New York, Harcourt, Brace, 1958, p. 607.

"Sun Our Father," *Forum,* XCVII (February, 1937), 116.

"In Memory of My Father (Campbell County, Tennessee)," *transition,* No. 26 (Spring, 1937), p. 7.

"Sunday: Outskirts of Knoxville, Tenn.," *New Masses,* XXIV (September 14, 1937), 22. Reprinted in Elizabeth Drew (ed.), *Directions in Modern Poetry.* New York, Norton, 1940, pp. 243-44.

"Lyrics" (11 sections), *Partisan Review,* IV (December, 1937), 40-43.

"Summer Evening," *Harper's Magazine,* CLXXVI (January, 1938), 209.

"Millions Are Learning How," *Common Sense,* VII (January, 1938), 27.

"Dixie Doodle," *Partisan Review,* IV (February, 1938), 8.

"I Had a Little Child," *Scholastic Review,* XXXIV (May 27, 1939), 27.

"Lullaby," in Seldon Rodman (ed.), *100 Modern Poets*. New York, Mentor Books, 1949, p. 100.

"Two Sonnets from a Dream," *Botteghe Oscure*, quaderno 5 (1950), pp. 336-37.

III.   *James Agee's Dramas and Films*

"Catched, a play in three scenes," *Phillips Exeter Monthly*, XXX (February, 1926), 87-97.

"In Vindication," *Phillips Exeter Monthly*, XXX (March, 1926), 122-26.

"Any Seventh Son," *Phillips Exeter Monthly*, XXXI (June, 1927), 107-109.

"The House," sketch for a scenario, in Horace Gregory (ed.), *New Letters in America*. New York, Norton, 1937, pp. 37-55.

"Man's Fate," sketch for a scenario, *Films*, I (1939), 51-60.

"Dedication Day," rough sketch for a moving picture, *Politics*, III (April, 1946), 121-25.

"Noa-Noa—A Fragment," in R. Hughes (ed.), *Film Book I*. New York, Grove Press, 1959, pp. 109-21. Incorporated in *Agee on Film*. Vol. II. New York, McDowell & Obolensky, 1960.

Agee on Film: Five Film Scripts (Vol. II):

———— "The Blue Hotel," written in 1948-49, under contract to Huntington Hartford, pp. 393-488.

———— "The African Queen," written in 1950, assisted by John Collier, John Huston, and Peter Viertel, released by United Artists, 1952, pp. 151-259.

———— "The Bride Comes to Yellow Sky," written in 1951–52 for Huntington Hartford, released by RKO under the title "Face to Face" in 1952, pp. 357-90.

———— "Noa-Noa," written in 1953, pp. 3-147.

———— "The Night of the Hunter," written in 1954, produced by Paul Gregory, released by United Artists, 1955, pp. 263-354.

James Agee also wrote a number of film scripts which have not been published:

"The Quiet One," commentary for a documentary film by Helen Levitt, released in 1948 (Museum of Modern Art Film Library, New York).

"Genghis Khan," a Filipino movie directed by Emmanuel Conde, released by Italian Film Exports, 1952.

"In the Street," shot by James Agee with Helen Levitt and Janice Loeb, 1952.

"Abraham Lincoln," written for Omnibus Television Series, 1953.

"White Mane," an adaptation from the French "Crin Blanc," distributed by Rembrandt Films and Contemporary Films, 1953.

"Green Magic," handled by Italian Film Export, New York, 1955.

"Williamsburg" (uncompleted), Colonial Williamsburg, Audio-visual Department, 1955.

"Tanglewood," on Berkshire Festival, in collaboration with Howard Taubman, bought by 20th Century-Fox.

IV.   James Agee's Non-Fiction

A. Books

Let Us Now Praise Famous Men, with Walker Evans. Boston, Houghton Mifflin, 1941, reprinted 1960.

B. Articles

"Extract From the Diary of a Disagreeable Young Man," *Phillips Exeter Monthly,* XXX (December, 1925), 62.

"Largest Class in History of School Grades," *Phillips Exeter Monthly,* XXXI (November, 1926), 48-52.

"To What Extent Do the Ramifications of International Trade and Commerce Affect the Political Relations Between the United States and the British Empire" (Brooks-Bryce Prize Essay), *Phillips Exeter Monthly,* XXXI (March, 1927), 135-40.

"Class History," *Phillips Exeter Monthly,* XXXII (June, 1932), 207-11.

"Housing," *Fortune,* VI (September, 1932), 74.

"Sheep and Shuttleworths," *Fortune,* VII (January, 1933), 43, 80.

"Strawberries," *Fortune,* VII (April, 1933), 64-69.

"$100,000 Worth," *Fortune,* VII (May, 1933), 58-66.

"Cincinnati Terminal," *Fortune,* VII (June, 1933), 72-76, 125.

"Baldness," *Fortune,* VIII (July, 1933), 52-55, 79-82.

"The Project is Important," *Fortune,* VIII (October, 1933), 81-97.

"Steel Rails," *Fortune,* VIII (December, 1933), 42-47, 153.

"Quinine to You," *Fortune,* IX (February, 1934), 76-86.

"Butler's Ball," *Fortune,* IX (March, 1934), 68-69.

"Cockfighting," *Fortune,* IX (March, 1934), 90-95, 146.

"U.S. Ambassadors," *Fortune,* IX (April, 1934), 108-22.

"Arbitrage," *Fortune,* IX (June, 1934), 93-97, 150-60.

"Roman Society," *Fortune,* X (July, 1934), 68-71, 144-50.

"Cabinet Changes," *Fortune,* X (July, 1934), 126-27.

"The American Roadside," *Fortune,* X (September, 1934), 53-63, 172-77.

"Drought," *Fortune,* X (October, 1934), 76-83.

"Illuminated Manuscripts," *Fortune,* X (December, 1934), 90-98.

"Glass," *Fortune,* XI (January, 1935), 48.

"T.V.A.," *Fortune,* XI (May, 1935), 93-98, 140-53.

"The Normandie," *Fortune,* XI (June, 1935), 84-88.

"Williamsburg Restored," *Fortune,* XII (July, 1935), 69-73.

"Saratoga," *Fortune,* XII (August, 1935), 63-69, 96-100.

"Hercules Powder," *Fortune,* XII (September, 1935), 57-62, 110-25.

"What D'You Mean, Modern?" *Fortune,* XII (November, 1935), 97-103, 164.

"U. S. Art: 1935," *Fortune,* XII (December, 1935), 68-75.

"The U.S. Commercial Orchid," *Fortune,* XII (December, 1935), 108-14, 126-29.

"Jewel Spread," *Fortune,* XIV (August, 1936), 70.

"Art for What's Sake," *New Masses,* XXI, no. 12 (December 15, 1936), 48.

"Posters by Cassandra," *Fortune,* XV (May, 1937), 120.

"Smoke," *Fortune,* XV (June, 1937), 100-102, 130.

"Six Days at Sea" *Fortune,* XVI (September, 1937), 117-20, 210-20.

"Three Tenant Families: A Selection," *Common Sense,* VIII (October, 1939), 9-12. (Partly incorporated in *Let Us Now Praise Famous Men,* 1941).

"Colon," *New Directions,* James Laughlin, ed., Norfolk, Conn., New Directions Pub. Co., 1936, 181-92. (Incorporated in *Let Us Now Praise Famous Men.*)

"Pseudo-Folk," *Partisan Review,* XI, no. 2 (Spring, 1944), 219-23.

"U.S. at War," *Time,* XLV (April 23, 1945), 1.

"Victory: The Peace," *Time,* XLVI (August 20, 1945), 19-21.

"New York, a Little Rain," *Time,* XLVI (October 1, 1945), 22-23.

"Europe: Autumn Story," *Time,* XLVI (October 15, 1945), 24-25.

"Godless Gotterdammerung," *Time,* XLVI (October 15, 1945), 62-64.

"The Nation," *Time,* XLVI (November 5, 1945), 22-24.

"Average Man," *Time,* XLVI (November 26, 1945), 58-60, 64.

"Voice of Reason," *Time,* XLVIII (August 26, 1946), 28.

"Syria: Triumph of Civilization," *Time,* XLVIII (September 9, 1946), 34.

"Russia: Last Mile," *Time,* XLVIII (September 9, 1946), 34.

"Food—Harvest Home," *Time,* XLVIII (September 23, 1946), 30.

"Great Britain," *Time,* XLVIII (September 23, 1946), 32-33.

"Great Britain: Beyond Silence," *Time,* XLVIII (October 7, 1946), 31.

"A Star in the Darkness," *Time,* XLIX (April 7, 1947), 55-56.

"Gandhi," *Politics,* V (Winter, 1948), 4.

"David Wark Griffith," *The Nation,* CLXVII (September 4, 1948), 264-66, reprinted in *Agee on Film* (I), 1958.

"Comedy's Greatest Era," *Life,* XXVII (September 3, 1949), 70-88, reprinted in *Agee on Film* (I), 1958.

"Religion and the Intellectuals," *Partisan Review,* XVII (February, 1950), 106-13.

"Undirectable Director," *Life,* XXIX (September 8, 1950), 128-45, reprinted in *Agee on Film* (I), 1958.

"Notes on Portfolio of Photographs 'Rapid Transit' by Walker Evans," *The Cambridge Review,* No. 5 (1956), p. 25.

"James Agee: By Himself," *Esquire,* LX (December, 1963), 149.

V. *James Agee's Reviews*

A. Theater

"Great New Actress" (Eileen Herlie), *Time,* XLVIII (September 30, 1946), 61.

"Olivier's Lear," *Time*, XLVIII (October 7, 1946), 56.
"The Ordeal of Eugene O'Neill," written with Louis
  Kronenberger, *Time*, XLVIII (October 21, 1946), 71-78
"Moon in Columbus" (on O'Neill's "A Moon for the
  Misbegotten"), *Time*, XLIX (March 3, 1947), 46.

B. Book Reviews

"Elmer Gantry," *Phillips Exeter Monthly*, XXXI (May,
  1927), 189-91.
"The Silver Sheet" (*God's Man* by Lynd Ward), *Harvard
  Advocate*, CXVI (April, 1930), 42.
"Suburban Cawdor" (*To the Gallows I Must Go* by T. S.
  Mathews), *Harvard Advocate*, CXVII (May, 1931), 86-88
"Abysmal Ah Youth" (*New England Holiday* by G. A.
  Smart), *Harvard Advocate*, CXVII (December, 1931), 28.
"Sins and Synonyms," *New Masses*, XXI (November 17,
  1936), 25.
"Sharecroppers Novels," *New Masses*, XXIII (June 8, 1937),
  23.

C. Book Reviews for *Time*

Vol. XXV: January 1, 1940, p. 47; January 8, 1940, pp.
  59-60; January 15, 1940, p. 68; January 22, 1940, p. 84;
  January 29, 1940, p. 72; February 5, 1940, pp. 64-67;
  February 12, 1940, p. 75; pp. 78, 79; p. 80; February 19,
  1940, p. 86; p. 90; February 26, 1940, pp. 91-92; March 4,
  1940, pp. 75-76; March 11, 1940, p. 84; pp. 87-88;
  March 18, 1940, p. 92; p. 96; April 1, 1940, p. 73; p. 75;
  April 8, 1940, pp. 86, 88; April 15, 1940, p. 100; p. 103;
  April 22, 1940, pp. 98-100; April 29, 1940, p. 88; May 6,
  1940, p. 91; May 13, 1940, pp. 94, 100, 102; May 20,
  1940, pp. 95-96; May 27, 1940, p. 93; p. 94; June 10, 1940,
  p. 90; June 17, 1940, pp. 88, 91; p. 92; June 24, 1940,
  pp. 94, 96.
Vol. XXXVI: July 1, 1940, p. 70; July 7, 1940, pp. 69, 71;
  July 22, 1940, pp. 80, 84; July 29, 1940, p. 60; p. 62; August
  5, 1940, pp. 68, 69; August 12, 1940, pp. 66-67; August
  19, 1940, p. 83; August 26, 1940, p. 60; September 2,
  1940, p. 64; December 2, 1940, pp. 80, 83; December 9,
  1940, p. 88; December 16, 1940, p. 102; December 30,
  1940, p. 58.

Vol. XXXVII: January 6, 1941, p. 59; January 13, 1941, pp. 76, 78-79; January 20, 1941, p. 80; February 3, 1941, p. 72; February 10, 1941, pp. 74-75; February 17, 1941, pp. 96, 98-99; February 24, 1941, pp. 98, 102; March 3, 1941, p. 86; March 10, 1941, pp. 90-94; March 17, 1941, pp. 94, 98, 100; March 24, 1941, pp. 90, 93; March 31, 1941, p. 74; April 7, 1941, p. 103; April 14, 1941, p. 99; April 21, 1941, pp. 104, 108; April 28, 1941, p. 91; May 12, 1941, p. 100; June 2, 1941, pp. 84, 86, 88; June 9, 1941; June 16, 1941, p. 88; June 23, 1941, p. 95; June 30, 1941, p. 86.

Vol. XXXVIII: July 7, 1941, p. 71; July 14, 1941, pp. 70, 72, 75; July 28, 1941, pp. 78-79; August 4, 1941, p. 72; August 11, 1941, p. 71; August 18, 1941, pp. 74-76; August 25, 1941, p. 79, September 1, 1941, p. 90; September 8, 1941, p. 71; September 15, 1941, p. 80; September 29, 1941, p. 91; October 13, 1941, p. 103; October 20, 1941, p. 108; November 24, 1941, pp. 110, 111; December 1, 1941, pp. 88, 91; December 15, 1941, pp. 108-14, "The Year in Books" (Agee and Whittaker Chambers); December 22, 1941, p. 64, "Literary Rotolactor" (on vanity publishing); December 29, 1941, p. 50.

Vol. XXXIX: January 5, 1942, pp. 68-71; January 12, 1942, pp. 75-76; January 19, 1942, pp. 78-79; January 26, 1942, p. 80; February 2, 1942, p. 74; February 9, 1942, pp. 75-76, "Half-century Score-board" (account of most popular books selection); February 16, 1942, pp. 90-92; February 23, 1942, p. 88; March 2, 1942, pp. 78-79; March 9, 1942, p. 84; March 16, 1942, p. 94; March 23, 1942, pp. 78, 79; March 30, 1942, pp. 79-80; April 6, 1942, p. 84; April 13, 1942, p. 104; April 20, 1942, p. 90; p. 96; April 27, 1942, p. 95; p. 96, "On the Skids" (review of little magazines); May 11, 1942, p. 95; p. 98; May 18, 1942, p. 86; May 25, 1942, p. 90; June 1, 1942, p. 82; June 8, 1942, pp. 90, 96; June 15, 1942, p. 84; pp. 87-88; June 22, 1942, p. 88; p. 91; June 29, 1942, pp. 74, 76.

Vol. XL: July 13, 1942, p. 88 (on war novels); July 20, 1942, p. 76; July 27, 1942, p. 80; August 2, 1942, p. 76; August 10, 1942, pp. 19, 91, 92; August 17, 1942, p. 78; August 24, 1942, p. 80; August 31, 1942, p. 100; December 21, 1942, p. 102, "The Year in Books" (Agee and other writers); December 28, 1942, p. 76.

Vol. XLI: January 4, 1943, p. 88; January 18, 1943, p. 100; February 1, 1943, pp. 84-86; pp. 85-87; February 8, 1943, pp. 88-91; February 15, 1943, pp. 94-95; February 22, 1943, pp. 88-90; March 1, 1943, pp. 83-84; March 15, 1943, pp. 78-80; March 22, 1943, pp. 74-75; March 29, 1943, pp. 69-71; pp. 71-72; April 5, 1943, pp. 100-101; April 26, 1943, pp. 100-101; June 7, 1943, pp. 96-107 (in collaboration with Harvey Breit).
Vol. XLII: August 16, 1943, p. 100; September 27, 1943, pp. 100-104; October 25, 1943, p. 98.
Vol. XLVII: February 25, 1946, pp. 98, 102-103; March 4, 1946, pp. 99, 104; March 25, 1946, pp. 102-106; April 1, 1946, p. 98, "Laureate of Youth" (on Housman), pp. 101-104.
Vol. XLIX: May 19, 1947, p. 108; "Milton is OK," p. 116.
New York Times Book Review, VII (December 13, 1953), 38: Review of *The Doctor and the Devils,* a movie script by Dylan Thomas.

D. Movie Reviews

"The Moving Picture," *Phillips Exeter Monthly,* XXX (March, 1936), 115-17.
Agee on Film: Reviews and Comments. Vol. I. New York, McDowell & Obolensky, 1958.

E. Movie Reviews for *Time*

Vol. XL: September 7, 1942, p. 104; September 14, 1942, p. 94; September 21, 1942, p. 69; September 28, 1942, pp. 82, 85, 92; October 5, 1942, pp. 84, 87; October 12, 1942, pp. 96-98; October 19, 1942, p. 96; October 26, 1942, pp. 96-98; November 2, 1942, pp. 96, 97; November 9, 1942, pp. 94, 96, 98; November 16, 1942, pp. 98, 99, 100; November 23, 1942, p. 109; November 30, 1942, pp. 94, 96; December 7, 1942, pp. 109-10; December 14, 1942, p. 109; December 21, 1942, p. 100.
Vol. XLII: July 12, 1943, p. 94; August 2, 1943, pp. 55-60, "For Whom?" (cover story on Ingrid Bergman); August 16, 1943, p. 93; September 6, 1943, pp. 94-95; September 13, 1943, pp. 94, 95; September 20, 1943, pp. 94, 96; September 27, 1943, pp. 92, 94, 97; October 4, 1943, pp. 92, 96; October 11, 1943, pp. 54, 56; October 25, 1943,

pp. 94-96; November 1, 1943, p. 54; November 15, 1943, p. 94; November 29, 1943, pp. 92-94; December 6, 1943, pp. 54-56; December 13, 1943, p. 92; December 20, 1943, pp. 54-61 (cover story on Greer Garson); December 27, 1943, pp. 90, 92.

Vol. XLIII: January 10, 1944, pp. 92-94; January 31, 1944, pp. 94, 96; February 28, 1944, pp. 93-94; March 6, 1944, pp. 94, 96; March 20, 1944, pp. 94-96; March 27, 1944, pp. 94, 96; April 3, 1944, pp. 92, 93; April 10, 1944, pp. 94-96; April 17, 1944, pp. 94, 96; April 24, 1944, pp. 94; May 1, 1944, pp. 90, 92; May 8, 1944, pp. 54, 56, 58; May 15, 1944, p. 54; May 22, 1944, pp. 93, 94, 96; May 29, 1944, pp. 93-96; June 5, 1944, pp. 94, 96; June 12, 1944, pp. 54, 56, 58; June 19, 1944, pp. 94, 96; June 26, 1944, pp. 94, 96.

Vol. XLIV: July 3, 1944, p. 88; July 10, 1944, pp. 94-96; July 17, 1944, pp. 94, 96; July 24, 1944, pp. 87, 89; July 31, 1944, pp. 50, 52; August 7, 1944, pp. 84, 88; August 14, 1944, p. 94; November 13, 1944, pp. 94, 96; November 20, 1944, p. 92; December 4, 1944, pp. 93-96; December 11, 1944, pp. 92-94; December 18, 1944, pp. 94-96; December 25, 1944, pp. 44-50.

Vol. XLV: January 1, 1945, pp. 40-41; January 8, 1945, pp. 39-40, 42, 44; January 15, 1945, pp. 92-96; January 22, 1945, pp. 91-92; January 29, 1945, pp. 94, 96; February 5, 1945, pp. 91, 92; February 12, 1945, pp. 52, 53; February 19, 1945, pp. 91, 92; February 26, 1945, pp. 92, 93; March 5, 1945, pp. 91, 92; March 12, 1945, pp. 94, 96; March 19, 1945, pp. 91, 92; March 26, 1945, pp. 94, 96; April 2, 1945, p. 90; April 9, 1945, pp. 90-96; April 16, 1945, pp. 92-96; April 30, 1945, pp. 89, 92; May 7, 1945, p. 94; May 14, 1945, pp. 93, 96; May 21, 1945, pp. 94-99; June 4, 1945, pp. 90, 92; June 25, 1945, pp. 88-90.

Vol. XLVI: July 30, 1945, pp. 96-100; August 6, 1945, pp. 98-100; August 13, 1945, pp. 94-96; August 20, 1945, pp. 98-101; August 27, 1945, pp. 94-99; September 3, 1945, pp. 92-96; September 10, 1945, pp. 98-100; September 17, 1945, pp. 95-98; September 24, 1945, pp. 56-58; October 1, 1945, p. 96; October 8, 1945, p. 96.

Vol. XLVII: April 1, 1946, pp. 93, 94, 96; April 8, 1946, pp. 56-60; April 29, 1946, pp, 94-95; May 6, 1946, pp.

96-101; May 13, 1946, pp. 98, 101; May 20, 1946, pp. 89, 90; May 27, 1946, p. 97; June 17, 1946, pp. 98, 101; June 24, 1946, p. 98.

Vol. XLVIII: August 19, 1946, p. 98; August 26, 1946, pp. 95, 96; September 2, 1946, pp. 91, 92; September 9, 1946, p. 100.

Vol. XLIX: February 3, 1947, pp. 92, 95; February 10, 1947, pp. 95-100; February 17, 1947, pp. 102, 104; February 24, 1947, pp. 106-10; March 3, 1947, pp. 81, 82; March 10, 1947, pp. 97, 98; March 17, 1947, pp. 100, 102; March 24, 1947, pp. 94, 96, 97, 98, 100; March 31, 1947, p. 99; April 7, 1947, pp. 99-102; April 14, 1947, pp. 100, 102; April 21, 1947, pp. 103-106; April 28, 1947, pp. 99-102; May 5, 1947, pp. 98-102; May 12, 1947, pp. 100-104; May 19, 1947, pp. 101-104; May 26, 1947, pp. 99-102; June 2, 1947, pp. 97-100; June 9, 1947, pp. 98-102; June 16, 1947, pp. 63-64; June 23, 1947, pp 93-94; June 30, 1947, pp. 95-96.

Vol. L: July 7, 1947, p. 66; July 14, 1947, pp. 90, 93; July 21, 1947; pp. 91-92; July 28, 1947, pp. 60-64; August 4, 1947, p. 76; August 11, 1947, pp. 95-97; August 18, 1947, pp. 95-96; August 25, 1947, pp. 88-90; September 1, 1947, pp. 80-82; September 8, 1947, pp. 98-102; September 15, 1947, pp. 101-104; September 22, 1947, pp. 97-100; September 29, 1947, pp. 99-102; October 6, 1947, pp. 101-103; October 13, 1947, pp. 105-108; October 20, 1947, pp. 101-102; October 27, 1947, pp. 99-100; November 3, 1947, pp. 99-101; December 15, 1947, pp. 103-106; December 22, 1947, pp. 80-82; December 29, 1947, pp. 62-63.

Vol. LI: January 5, 1948, pp. 71-72; January 12, 1948, pp. 52-56; January 26, 1948, pp. 95-96; February 2, 1948, pp. 80, 82; February 9, 1948, pp. 93, 96; February 16, 1948, pp. 99-102; March 1, 1948, pp. 84, 86; March 8, 1948, pp. 104, 107; March 15, 1948, pp. 100-104; March 22, 1948, pp. 96, 99, 100; March 29, 1948, pp. 98-102; April 5, 1948, pp. 94-98; April 12, 1948, pp. 100-104; April 19, 1948, pp. 91, 96; May 10, 1948, pp. 100-104; May 17, 1948, pp. 102-108; May 24, 1948, pp. 96-102; May 31, 1948, pp. 86-89; June 7, 1948, pp. 98, 102; June 14, 1948, p. 98; June 21, 1948, pp. 96-100; June 28, 1948, pp 54-62 (also cover story on Jean Simmons).

Vol. LII: July 5, 1948, pp. 60, 62; July 12, 1948, pp. 82, 85;
July 19, 1948, pp. 98-102; July 26, 1948, pp. 65, 66;
August 2, 1948, pp. 72-74; August 9, 1948, pp. 74-75, 77;
August 16, 1948, pp. 90-94; August 30, 1948, p. 72;
September 6, 1948, pp. 86, 88; September 13, 1948, pp.
102, 106; September 20, 1948, pp. 100, 106; October
18, 1948, pp. 103-106; October 25, 1948, pp. 102-105;
November 1, 1948, p. 94; November 8, 1948, pp. 102-103.

F. Movie Reviews for *The Nation*

Vol. CLV: December 26, 1942, p. 727.
Vol. CLVI: January 23, 1943, p. 139; February 20, p. 283;
March 20, pp. 426, 462; May 1, p. 642; May 22,
p. 749; June 12, p. 844.
Vol. CLVII: July 17, p. 82; July 24, p. 108; September 4,
p. 175; September 25, p. 360; October 23, p. 480; October
30, p. 509; November 6, p. 563; November 13, p. 565;
November 20, p. 593; December 4, p. 677; December 18,
p. 741; December 25, p. 768.
Vol. CLVIII: January 1, 1944, p. 23; January 8, p. 52;
January 15, p. 81; January 22, p. 108; January 29, p. 137;
February 5, p. 167; February 12, p. 197; February 26,
p. 261; March 4, p. 288; March 11, p. 316; March 18, p.
344; March 25, p. 375; April 1, p. 401; April 8, p. 428;
April 15, p. 456; May 6, p. 549; May 13, p. 577; May 20, p.
605; May 27, p. 634; June 3, p. 661; June 10, p. 688;
June 17, p. 716; June 24, p. 743.
Vol. CLIX: July 1, p. 24; July 8, p. 53; July 15, p. 81; July
22, p. 107; July 29, p. 137; August 5, p. 165; August 19,
p. 171; September 16, p. 334; September 30, p. 361;
October 7, p. 389; October 14, p. 445; November 4, p. 569;
November 18, p. 624; November 25, p. 670; December
2, p. 698; December 9, p. 725; December 16, p. 753;
December 23, p. 781.
Vol. CLX: January 6, 1945, p. 24; January 20, p. 80; January
27, p. 110; February 3, p. 136; February 10, p. 166;
February 17, p. 192; February 24, p. 230; March 3, p. 257;
March 11, p. 285; March 17, p. 314; March 24, p. 342;
March 31, p. 370; April 7, p. 395; April 14, p. 425; April
21, p. 469; April 28, p. 497; May 12, p. 554; May 19,
p. 579; May 26, p. 608; June 7, p. 657.

Vol. CLXI: July 21, p. 67; August 11, p. 141; August 25, p. 189; September 15, p. 264; September 29, p. 321; October 13, p. 385; October 27, p. 441; November 10, p. 506; November 24, p. 562; December 22, p. 697.

Vol. CLXII: January 5, 1946, p. 24; January 19, p. 81; February 16, p. 205; March 2, p. 269; March 23, p. 354; April 13, p. 443; April 27, p. 516; May 11, p. 580; May 25, p. 636; June 8, p. 201; June 22, p. 765.

Vol. CLXIII: July 6, p. 25; July 20, p. 80; August 3, p. 135; August 10, p. 165; August 17, p. 193; August 31, p. 249; September 14, p. 305; September 28, p. 361; October 12, p. 417; October 26, p. 482; November 9, p. 536; December 7, p. 672; December 14, p. 708; December 28, p. 766.

Vol. CLXIV: January 25, 1947, p. 108; February 1, p. 134; February 15, p. 193; March 1, pp. 257-59; March 22, pp. 339, 340; April 12, p. 433; May 10, pp. 551-53; May 31, p. 665; June 14, p. 723; June 21, p. 749; June 28, p. 778.

Vol. CLXV: July 5, p. 23; July 12, p. 51; July 19, p. 79; August 2, p. 129; August 16, p. 172; August 30, p. 209; September 13, p. 264; September 20, p. 290; September 27, p. 320; December 13, p. 655; December 27, p. 706.

Vol. CLXVI: January 10, 1948, p. 53; January 31, p. 136; February 14, p. 191; April 24, p. 449; May 22, p. 584; June 19, p. 697.

G. Miscellaneous Movie Reviews

"The Marx Brothers," *Films in Review,* I (July-August, 1950), 25-29.

"Sunset Boulevard," *Sight and Sound,* XIX (November, 1950), 283-85.

VI. *James Agee's Letters*

James Agee and Dwight Macdonald: Exchange of Letters. Agee's reply, *The Nation,* CLVI (1943), 873-74 (about Agee's review of the film "Mission to Moscow").

Letters of James Agee to Father Flye. New York, George Braziller, 1962.

Secondary Sources

I. Bibliographies

Fabre, Genevieve. "A Bibliography of the Works of James
Agee," *Bulletin of Bibliography*, XXIV, no. 7
(May-August, 1965), 145-48, 163-66.

II. Biographies

Evans, Walker, "James Agee in 1936," *Atlantic Monthly*,
CCVI (July, 1960), 74-75. Reprinted in *Let Us Now
Praise Famous Men*, 1960 edition.
Huston, John. Foreword to *Agee on Film*. Vol. II. New York,
McDowell & Obolensky, 1960, pp. ix-x.

III. Critical Books and Articles on James Agee

Alpert, Hollis. "The Terror on the River," *Saturday Review*,
XXXVIII (August 13, 1955), 21.
Auden, W. H. "A Letter to the Editors of *The Nation*,"
The Nation, CLIX (October 14, 1944). Reprinted in *Agee
on Film* (Vol. I).
Barker, George. "Three Tenant Families," *The Nation*,
CLIII (September 27, 1941), 282.
Bazelon, David T. "Agee on Film," *The Village Voice*, IV
(December 24, 1958), 12, 14-15.
Behar, Jack. *James Agee: The World of His Work*.
Unpublished doctoral dissertation, Ohio State University,
1963.
Bingham, R. "Short of a Distant Goal," *The Reporter*, XXVII
(October 25, 1962), 54f.
Breit, Harvey. "Cotton Tenantry," *The New Republic*, CV
(September 15, 1941), 348-50.
Burger, Nash K. "A Story to Tell: Agee, Wolfe, Faulkner,"
South Atlantic Quarterly, LXIII (Autumn, 1964), 32-43.
Chase, Richard. "Sense and Sensibility," *The Kenyon Review*,
Autumn, 1951, pp. 688-91.
Croce, Arlene. "Hollywood the Monolith," *Commonweal*,
LXIX (January 23, 1959), 430-33.
da Fonte, Durant. "James Agee: The Quest for Identity,"
Tennessee Studies in Literature, VIII (Winter, 1963),
25-37.

Dempsey, D. "Praise of Him was Posthumous," *Saturday Review,* XIV (August 11, 1962), 24-25.

Dunlea, W. "Agee and the Writer's Vocation," *Commonweal,* LXXVI (September 7, 1962), 499-500.

Dupee, F. W. "Pride of Maturity," *The Nation,* CLXXII (April 28, 1951), 400-401.

Fiedler, Leslie. "Encounter with Death," *The New Republic,* CXXXVII (December 9, 1957), 25-26.

Flye, Father James Harold. Introduction to *Letters of James Agee to Father Flye.* New York, George Braziller, 1962, pp. 11-13.

Frohock, W. M. "James Agee: The Question of Unkept Promise," *Southwest Review,* XLII (Summer, 1957), 221-29.

————. "James Agee—The Question of Wasted Talent," in *The Novel of Violence in America.* Boston, Beacon Press, 1964, pp. 212-30.

Goodman, Paul. "Review of *Let Us Now Praise Famous Men,*" *Partisan Review,* LX (January-February, 1942), 86-87.

Gregory, Horace. "The Beginning of Wisdom," *Poetry,* XXXXVI (April 1935), 48-51.

Harker, Jonathan. "Review of *Agee on Film:* Volume II," *Film Quarterly,* XII (Spring, 1959), 58-59.

Hatch, Robert. "Films," *The Nation,* CLXXXI (October 15, 1955), 328-29.

Hays, Richard. "James Agee: Rhetoric of Splendor," *Commonweal,* LXVIII (September 12, 1958), 591-92

Hicks, Granville. "Suffering Face of the Rural South," *Saturday Review,* XLIII (September 10, 1960), 19-20.

Holder, Alan. "Encounter in Alabama: Agee and the Tenant Farmer," *Virginia Quarterly Review,* XXXXII, no. 2 (Spring, 1966), 189-206.

Holland, Norman. "Agee on Film: Reviewer Re-Viewed," *The Hudson Review,* XII (Spring, 1959), 148-51.

Howe, Irving. Radio broadcast on *A Death in the Family* WGBH-FM (Boston), February 2, 1958.

Kauffman, Stanley. "A Life in Reviews," *The New Republic,* CXXXIX (December 1, 1958), 18-19.

Kazin, Alfred. *Contemporaries.* Boston, Little, Brown, 1962, pp. 185-87.

Kirstein, Lincoln. "First Poems," *The New Republic,* LXXXII (February 27, 1935), 80-81.

Kramer, Victor A. "James Agee Papers at the University of Texas," *Library Chronicle of the University of Texas,* VIII, no. 2, 33-36.

Lakin, R. D. "D. W.'s: The Displaced Writer in America," *Midwest Quarterly,* IV (Winter, 1963), 295-303.

Larsen, Erling. "Let Us Not Now Praise Ourselves," *Carleton Miscellany,* II (Winter, 1961), 86-97.

Levin, Meyer. "Abraham Lincoln Through the Picture Tube," *The Reporter,* VIII (April 14, 1953), 31-33.

Macdonald, Dwight. "Death of a Poet," *New Yorker,* XXXIII (November 16, 1957), 224ff. Reprinted in *Against the American Grain,* New York, Vintage Books, 1965, 143-66.

————. "James Agee, Some Memories and Letters," *Encounter,* XIX (December, 1962), 73-84

————. "On Chaplin, Verdoux and Agee," *Esquire,* LXIII (April, 1965), 18ff.

Morrison, Theodore. "Modern Poets," *The Atlantic Bookshelf,* CLV (March, 1935), 10-12.

Mosel, Tad, and Philip Reisman, Jr. *All the Way Home* New York, Avon Books, 1963, pp. 15-162.

Mills, C. Wright. "Sociological Poetry," *Politics,* V (Spring, 1948), 125-26.

Ohlin, P. H. *Agee.* New York, Obolensky, 1966.

Oulahan, Richard. "A Cult Grew around a Many-Sided Writer," *Life,* LV (November 1, 1963), 69-72.

Pechter, William S. "On Agee on Film," *Sight and Sound,* XXXIII (Summer, 1964), 148-53.

Phelps, Robert. "James Agee," in *Letters of James Agee to Father Flye.* New York, George Braziller, 1962, pp. 1-9.

Phillipson, J. S. "Character, Theme, and Symbol in *The Morning Watch,*" *Western Humanities Review,* XV (Autumn, 1961), 359-67.

Poster, William S. "Man in the Movies," *Commentary,* XXVI (December, 1958), 176-79.

Pryce-Jones, Alan. Preface to *The Morning Watch.* New York, Ballantine Books, 1966.

Rodman, Seldon. "The Poetry of Poverty," *Saturday Review of Literature,* XXIV (August 23, 1941), 6.

Roe, Michael M., Jr. "A Point of Focus in James Agee's *A*

Death in the Family," Twentieth Century Literature, XII
   (October, 1966), 149-53.

Roud, Richard. "Face to Face: James Agee," Sight and
   Sound, XXVIII (Spring, 1959), 98-100.

Seib, Kenneth. A Death in the Family: A Critical
   Commentary, New York, Study*Master Publications, 1965.

Seldes, Gilbert. "John Huston in Darkest Africa," The
   Saturday Review, XXV (February 23, 1952), 30.

Simon, John. "Let Us Now Praise James Agee," The
   Mid-Century, XV, no. 6 (November, 1959), 17-22.

————. "The Preacher Turns Practitioner," The Mid-Century,
   XVII, no. 27 (Summer, 1961), 18-21.

Stevenson, David L. "Tender Anguish," The Nation,
   CLXXXV (December 14, 1957), 460-61.

Taylor, John Russell. "Review of Agee on Films: Volume
   II," Sight and Sound, XXX (Winter, 1960-61), 46-47.

Trilling, Lionel. "Greatness with One Fault in It," The
   Kenyon Review, IV (Winter, 1942), 99-102.

————. "The Story and the Novel," The Griffin, no. 7,
   (January, 1958), pp. 4-12.

————. "An American Classic," The Mid-Century, no. 16
   (September, 1960), 3-10.

Updike, John. "No Use Talking," New Republic, CXXXXVII
   (August 13, 1962), 23-24.

Watkins, Vernon. "Film Chronicle," The Hudson Review,
   XIV (Summer, 1961), 270-83.

Weales, Gerald. "The Accidents of Compassion," The
   Reporter, XVII (December 12, 1957), 42-43.

————. "The Critic in Love," The Reporter, XIX
   (December 25, 1958), 38-39.

————. "The Film Writer," Commonweal, LXXII (April
   29, 1960), 134-35.

Wensberg, Erik. "I've Been Reading," Columbia University
   Forum, III (Fall, 1960), 38-42.

The reader is also urged to listen to Samuel Barber's
   Knoxville: Summer of 1915, for Soprano and Orchestra.
   The only currently available recording is by Eleanor
   Steber, soprano, and William Strickland conducting the
   Dumbarton Oaks Chamber Orchestra (Columbia ML
   5843).

IV. Other Works Consulted

Aaron, Daniel. *Writers on the Left.* New York, Avon Books, 1965.

Arnheim, Rudolf. "A Bird's Eye View of Film," remarks delivered at the second performance of Moving Images, a film series at the University of Virginia, November 18, 1961, personal notes.

Baldwin, James. *Notes of a Native Son.* Boston, Beacon Press, 1955.

Bluestone, George. *Novels into Film.* Baltimore, The Johns Hopkins Press, 1957.

Chase, Richard. *The American Novel and its Tradition.* New York, Doubleday, 1957.

Conrad, Joseph. Preface to *The Nigger of the "Narcissus."* New York, Doubleday, 1914.

Cowley, Malcolm. *The Literary Situation.* New York, Viking, 1958.

Greenburg, Clement. "Avant-Garde and Kitsch," in Bernard Rosenberg and David Manning White (eds.), *Mass Culture: The Popular Arts in America.* Glencoe, Ill., The Free Press, 1957, pp. 98-107.

Hofstadter, Richard. *The Age of Reform.* New York, Vintage Books, 1955.

Houston, Penelope. *The Contemporary Cinema.* Baltimore, Penguin Books, 1963, pp. 22, 46.

James, Henry. *Partial Portraits.* London, Macmillan, 1888.
————. *The Art of the Novel.* New York, Charles Scribner's Sons, 1934.

Jarrell, Randall. *Poetry and the Age.* New York, Vintage Books, 1953,

Kazin, Alfred. *On Native Grounds.* New York, Doubleday, 1956.

McLuhan, Marshall. *Understanding Media: The Extensions of Man.* New York, McGraw-Hill, 1966.

Marcosson, Isaac. *Adventures in Interviewing.* New York, John Lane Company, 1920.

Montagu, Ashley. "The Natural Superiority of Women," *Saturday Review,* XXXV (March 1, 1952), 28ff.

Pound, Ezra. *Literary Essays of Ezra Pound.* ed. and intro. T. S. Eliot. Norfolk, Conn., New Directions, 1954.

index

173